RARE
LIKE US

*From Losing My Dad to Finding Myself
in a Family Plagued By Genetic Disease*

TAYLOR KANE

To my mom, Diane, who always pushes me to be the best version of myself.

To my brother, Matthew, who always lends me a helping hand, and who is kind enough never to brag that his grades are better than mine.

To my stepdad, Keith Johnson, who treats Matthew and me as if we were his own by giving us unconditional love, support and encouragement, and who constantly makes me laugh.

To my rare friends—Shira, Seth, Stefanos—all incredible advocates who remind me how important it is to live in the present.

To my rare "moms" and "dads" (and sisters) —Janice, Bob, Monica, Karen, Elisa, Jesse, Jenn, Lisa, Lindsey, Stephanie, Carrie, Andra and many more— who have taken me under their wings and been amazing mentors.

In Loving Memory of My Dad, John Joseph Kane

CONTENTS

Preface ix

PART ONE 1

1. *Always in Our Hearts* 3

2. *The Nightmare Begins* 9

3. *Our New Normal* 15

4. *The Magic Kingdom* 21

5. *Running Away* 27

6. *Firemen and Fundraisers* 35

7. *Making Mountains Out of Molehills* 39

8. *When It Rains, It Pours* 45

9. *The Power of Denial* 51

10. *The Run for ALD* 59

11. *Judgers and Judges* 65

12. *In the Eye of the Storm* 73

13. *Life in a Bubble* 79

14. *My Fifth Summer* 85

15. *The Beginning of the End* 89

16. *My Dad Gets His Wings* 95

PART TWO 111

17. *Coping and Moving On* 113

18. *Children Grieve Too* 117

19. *Finding My Voice* 125

20. *Taking the Bad with the Good* 131

21. *Distressed Genes* 137

22. Telling My Story 143

23. The Power of Volunteering 153

24. Anyone Can Be a Hero 159

25. Reaching Out 167

26. Staking Out My Future 173

27. Remember the Girls 179

Epilogue 185

Resources 191

About the Author 195

PREFACE

There's a website that calculates which words you use most often on Facebook. When I tried it, I discovered that the word I used most was "rare." This may seem a little strange, but I can't say that it really surprised me. After all, for a twenty year old, I think I've had a pretty rare life—and I mean that literally. My father was diagnosed with a rare genetic disease when I was three years old and passed away from that disease when I was five. Shortly thereafter, I learned I was a carrier of the same rare disease and that I would have a fifty percent chance of passing the disease on to my children. Over the years, I've become a fierce advocate for awareness of rare diseases, traveling across the country to speak at rare disease conferences and leading groups of rare disease patients and their families to advocate for pro-rare disease legislation on Capitol Hill. When I was eighteen years old, I founded my own nonprofit organization to unite and support female carriers of rare genetic diseases. And finally, just this year, a college friend and I started a new organization called—you guessed it—RARE, an acronym for Research-Advocate-Reform-Educate, to raise awareness of rare diseases on campus.

Now that you know where I got the title for this book, I'd like to tell you why I wrote it. First, and most importantly, I felt I could help others by sharing what I've learned growing up in a family plagued by a rare disease—one in which I not only watched my father decline and then pass away after being ravaged both physically and mentally, but where other extended family members, including my dad's identical twin brother, suffered the same or similar fates or, like me, are carriers of the deadly disease. The lessons I've learned throughout this ordeal have helped me immeasurably in my quest to come to grips with my father's death and move forward with my life. I believe they could benefit not only rare disease patients and their families, but anyone who has suffered the loss of a loved one or has had to face an uncertain medical future or any other type of adversity, for that matter, particularly at a young age.

Another one of my reasons for writing this book was to bring attention to the realities associated with rare diseases and the challenging issues that face the rare disease community as a whole. Since I address this topic throughout the book, I will not go into detail here except to point out that if you are interested in learning more about rare diseases or would like to find out how you can support the cause, I have included an appendix at the back of this book which lists a number of fantastic nonprofit organizations that advocate for those with rare diseases in the United States and in other countries.

Finally, I decided to write this book to honor my dad—my hero—John Joseph Kane. My dad was born and raised in South Philadelphia. He grew up in a small row home where he shared an attic bedroom with his identical twin brother. Beginning in high school, he worked as a longshoreman, eventually paying his way through college and then law school. As a lawyer, he was a client favorite, representing working-class men and women who could not navigate the legal system themselves. My dad was down-to-earth, gregarious, kind, compassionate, and had an unstoppable sense of humor. He was a diehard fan of all of the Philadelphia sports teams. He was also an amazing father. He loved life and he died far too young.

I wish I knew more about my dad's life before he was diagnosed with adrenoleukodystrophy. But sadly, most of my memories of my dad involve hospital beds and wheelchairs and feeding tubes and Hoyer lifts and catheters and hospice nurses and so on. Still, I have many happy memories of the time I spent with him during his illness. We laughed and had fun together despite all of the hardships. My dad was an eternal optimist and maintained his cheerful disposition and good humor until the very end.

Because it was important to me that this book be factually accurate, I describe many of the physical and cognitive symptoms he experienced and the manner in which they affected us as a family. While some might consider these details too private or embarrassing to be put into writing, I disagree, and I know my dad would too. Medical symptoms should not have to be hidden as shameful secrets. My dad was not his symptoms; suffering them was not his choice. Indeed, many of the greatest difficulties we confronted as a family stemmed from others who either could not face his symptoms or who pretended they didn't exist. (One word of caution to those who have adrenoleukodystrophy or have a family member with the condition: adrenoleukodystrophy manifests differently in different people. My dad's experience with the disease was unique to him—even his twin brother had vastly different symptoms. Accordingly, my dad's battle with this disease is not in any way predictive of anyone else's journey.)

So, how did I write this book given that I was still very young at the time many of the events occurred? To begin with, I interviewed my mother, Diane Kane, extensively. Although we had discussed many of these events on numerous occasions while I was growing up, she and I re-explored her memories in great detail and reviewed her personal diaries, as well as medical reports, legal documents, newspaper articles, and letters she had accumulated in order to corroborate her recollections. Since part one of this book relates to incidents that occurred before my sixth birthday, it contains more of my mom's feelings and perceptions—exactly as she relayed them to me—than it does my own. Since she served as my dad's primary caregiver, I felt that including her point of view would be both illuminating and beneficial to others in similar situations. Plus, I learned a lot from her too.

In addition to my mom, I also interviewed a number of other people who were close to my dad at the time and who had specific knowledge of the material facts referred to in this book. Finally, I relied upon my own memories and my daily journal, which I have kept since I was in sixth grade. Part two of this book only includes events that I clearly remember and is essentially my personal memoir, written from my perspective as a young girl, as a teenager, and finally as a young adult.

With the exception of family members and close friends, I have changed the names of some of the individuals mentioned in this book, as well as the details of certain events, to protect anonymity.

PART ONE

In the United States, a disease is considered to be "rare" if it affects less than 200,000 people. Cumulatively, however, rare diseases are not really that rare. At last count there are more than 7,000 rare diseases that affect over 25 million Americans. One in every ten of us is born with some type of rare disorder. Unfortunately, the overwhelming majority of rare disorders do not have even a single FDA-approved treatment. Doctors may be unfamiliar with rare diseases they haven't seen before; accordingly, there is often a significant delay before a patient is accurately diagnosed. In some cases, this delay can have devastating consequences.

Adrenoleukodystrophy, more commonly referred to as ALD, is a particularly deadly rare genetic disease that affects approximately one in every 18,000 people worldwide. It is what is known as a X-linked disease, meaning it is passed from parent to child through a defect on the X chromosome. Because males only have one X chromosome, they are typically more severely affected by the disease than females, who have two X chromosomes (one of which is unaffected and compensates for the genetic defect on the other). Often, they are diagnosed as young boys between the ages of four and ten. These previously healthy boys typically begin to exhibit behavioral problems, memory lapses, and difficulties with reading, writing, and comprehension. The disease quickly progresses as the myelin sheath in their brains deteriorates, and they experience seizures, loss of muscle control, blindness, deafness, and dementia.

By this time, it is usually too late for effective treatment—a risky stem cell trans- plant—and the disease often results in death, usually within several years of diagnosis.

Males with the defective gene who escape this childhood form of ALD may still be stricken with symptoms as adults. Most adult males with the disease experience difficulty walking and many eventually become wheelchair bound. Others, like my dad, experience the same devastating physical and mental deterioration as boys, lapsing into a vegetative state and dying shortly thereafter. There is no known cure for men with ALD.

Experimental treatments for ALD, particularly gene therapy, appear quite promising, at least for young boys with the disease.

CHAPTER ONE

Always in Our Hearts

Diane Schmauder Kane is with Taylor Kane.

June 18, 2016 · Mount Laurel

Jack,

It's been almost fifteen years since you were diagnosed with ALD and we learned that you wouldn't be around to see our children graduate kindergarten, much less grow to adulthood. I promised you that I would do my best to raise them without you, although I wasn't sure exactly how I would do it. Well, guess what? I'm halfway there . . . Our baby girl graduated high school today!!

I wish you could have been there to see her walk across the football field and receive her diploma. She is everything a person could hope for in a daughter—smart, funny, independent, compassionate, and full of life. She is so much like you in so many ways: the way she makes instant friends with everyone she meets; the way she talks nonstop and entertains people with her self-deprecating sense of humor; and the way she is always the first to reach out to others who have suffered a loss or a tragedy. Like you, she's always had an uncanny ability to comfort people, even at a very young age. Back when she was in fifth grade, she received an award from a teacher who wrote: "After losing my own mother to cancer one year ago, Taylor Kane has impacted my life with her smile, authentic nature, and remarkable strength . . . I appreciate her for the inspiration she has given me when it was hard to get out of bed most mornings, and I will always remember her . . ." Since I have heard similar sentiments from many others over the last fifteen years, I can't help but believe she is truly something special—like you were, of course.

She also has talents that neither of us had. She is an amazing public speaker who can get up on a stage before hundreds of people and make them laugh or cry without ever missing a beat. Even better, she always stands up for what she believes regardless of the cost, and makes it her mission to try to make the world a better place—whether it be by visiting with Alzheimer's patients, volunteering at a camp for grieving children, fighting for equal rights for women, or advocating for ALD newborn screening. In fact, when New Jersey finally does begin screening newborns for ALD and affected boys' lives are saved as a result, this will be in large part due to her hard work and unwavering commitment to honor your memory. You would be so proud!!!

In less than two months, she'll be headed off to college in Washington, D.C., where I'm sure she will continue to make her mark, and the house will be eerily quiet (while your son is extremely smart, he is not much of a talker). Although it feels like such a long time since you've been gone, it also seems as though our little girl has grown up in the blink of an eye.

I know you would have loved to be around to share the special milestones in her life, especially this big one, but you'll be glad to know she has always felt that you were with her in spirit, watching over her and guiding her. That belief has made her strong, compassionate, and determined to live her life to the fullest. She is so very excited to go off to college in D.C. and begin the new journey that lies ahead of her. And I am so grateful to have had the opportunity to raise this extraordinary girl who has so much to offer the world, and who I know will go on to do great things.

Always,

Diane

My mom posted this letter to my dad on Facebook a little more than three years ago—the day after my high school graduation and a week before my eighteenth birthday. I know, she makes me sound like some kind of saint, right? I'm obviously not, of course, but I guess that's just what moms do. Her post reminds me, though, of how far we've come—my mom, my younger brother Matthew, and I—since my dad was diagnosed with ALD. It hasn't always been easy, not for any of us.

I'm sure it must have been hardest on my mom, especially at the beginning—having to take care of my dad while raising two toddlers and holding down a full-time job as an attorney. And then, of course, enduring the pressure and responsibility of parenting us throughout our remaining childhood years without the support of the man she had counted on being there through it all. But I have to hand it to her, she never complained or felt sorry for herself. She always told us, "You just have to make the best of what you have." And she did. She insisted that we do it too.

There were plenty of fights—even screaming matches—between my mom and I as I was growing up, especially when she would shut off my cell phone after I had done something that she considered particularly unacceptable, like staying out way past curfew or leaving the basement in a complete state of disarray after a sleepover. (I have to admit, I could be a bit trying on occasion.) But there were far more good times than bad, and I always knew that my mom just wanted the best for me. She was the glue that held our family together through everything.

I think losing my dad was pretty hard on my brother Matthew too. It's hard to tell with him; he's always been extremely quiet and introspective. He was only one year old when my dad got sick and doesn't remember him ever being able to walk or talk. But after my dad died, when Matthew was a little bit older, he would cling to my mom, afraid of losing her too. I know how he felt.

Growing up, Matthew spent most of his time in his bedroom playing video games, probably trying to zone out all of the outspoken females around him (not only my mom and me, but our various babysitters and caretakers over the years). He was always smart as a whip, though, eventually graduating high school tied for first in his class despite studying very little—at least compared to how much I had to study. Everyone thinks he resembles my dad in physical appearance, and I do too. My mom says Matthew is much more handsome.

As for me—like my mom wrote in her Facebook post, I definitely inherited my dad's personality. My mom used to say that I was so much like my dad it was scary. "Two peas in a pod," she would remark whenever I did something particularly unique that reminded her of him. For instance, she once told me that when I was around two years old, after she had taken me to the supermarket with her a few times, by the third or fourth trip I demanded to get out of the shopping cart so I could say hello to all of the checkout clerks in the store, each of whom I already knew by name. My mom was flabbergasted by this—she was always so focused on her shopping and her internal to-do list, she sheepishly admitted, that she barely remembered the clerks' faces, much less what was printed on their name tags—even after having shopped there for the last five years.

"You're a people-person, just like your father," she told me. "He never forgot a name or a face. He and I were on vacation in Fort Lauderdale once, and as we pulled into a hotel parking lot, your dad greeted the parking lot attendant by name and gave him a big hug. When I asked him later how he knew the man, your dad said that he had parked at the same hotel ten years earlier and that he had had a conversation with that very same attendant, and that *of course* he remembered his name. I couldn't believe it."

According to my mom, my dad also had an extraordinary ability to put himself into other people's shoes, especially those who had experienced some sort of loss. "He had a unique knack for being able to understand and sympathize with their feelings and bring them comfort," she recalled, smiling. "People always told him he should have been a priest. He used to read the obituaries and then go to the funerals of people he barely knew. He had some inexplicable need to try to console the grieving family members, and he was incredibly good at it. Somehow, he was always able to bring a smile to the faces of even those people who were the most distraught. Your father probably went to three or four funerals every month. Personally, I thought it was kind of strange. I never completely understood him."

Like my dad, I suppose I have always been very empathetic too, somehow drawn to other people who seem sad or lost. Even adults would confide in me when I was quite young, perhaps knowing that my father had died and somehow sensing I could understand their pain. I stayed after school plenty of times to commiserate with teachers who would tell me of a parent's cancer diagnosis, a family problem, or some other hardship. When friends' grandparents or great-grandparents passed away, I seemed to be the one my friends turned to for comfort and guidance. My mom would get inevitably get calls from the concerned parents asking if I could possibly accompany their child to the funeral. (After all, I had pretty much become an expert in attending funerals by then.) "Two peas in a pod," my mom would say, shaking her head. But it came naturally to me, just as it did to my dad.

The loss of my dad has had an enormous impact on my life. Although he passed away when I was only five-and-a-half years old, I still have vivid memories of him before he got sick. I clearly recall him playing with me in our backyard and helping me down the slide. I remember him lifting me up in the ocean so the waves wouldn't knock me over. I remember his light blue eyes and his crooked smile, and the way he was always laughing. I even remember the time he took me to the mall and I ran away when he wasn't looking. Mall security found me thirty minutes later sitting under a jewelry rack playing with the earrings at Claire's Boutique (which, looking back, is not surprising given my affinity for sparkling accessories). My mom was furious with me when she found out, but not my dad—he rarely ever got mad.

I still think about my dad every day, all these years later. But thinking about him doesn't make me sad anymore like it used to. I guess I've learned the art of acceptance. Now when I think of him, I feel an overwhelming sense of joy and gratitude that I had him for a father, even for such a short time. I'm not sure exactly how or when my feelings changed, but they did. Remembering him, seeing a picture of him, or listening to his voice on a cassette tape—they all make me smile now (although sometimes in a wistful sort of way).

For years after my dad died, I struggled with recurrent feelings of anxiety, depression, and sometimes a sense of derealization—never understanding exactly how I fit into this world and what my true purpose for being here was. But now I know. The answer was inside me the whole time. And it all goes back to the lessons I learned *from* my dad—and those I learned *from losing* him.

CHAPTER TWO

The Nightmare Begins

Seventeen Years Earlier

It all started as a bunch of little things. Things so small and seemingly insignificant that my mom thought she must be imagining that there might be a problem. But during that summer of 2001, my dad, who was normally compulsively neat and organized, stopped noticing when the pencils faced different directions in the desk drawer and when the fringe on the oriental rug did not lay perfectly flat. At least, he stopped commenting on it and did nothing to fix it. There were times when he would leave mail sitting on the kitchen counter; a few times he got ready for work without making the bed.

He also stopped being as frugal with money. My dad had always been extremely thrifty, obsessively checking the math on every receipt to make sure he wasn't overcharged—even clipping coupons to make sure he got the best deal. But when my mom told him she wanted a minivan so she could get my brother and me in and out of the car more easily, he bought the first Ford Windstar they looked at without even haggling over the sticker price.

At first, my mom was relieved—actually elated—by these apparent changes in my dad's personality. Things were so much easier, she found, when my dad wasn't inspecting every nook and cranny for dust and scrutinizing every shopping receipt.

Then she noticed more personality changes. My dad seemed a little quieter and interacted with people less at social gatherings. Sometimes he would sit off in a corner by himself just staring into space. He also began waking up later, on occasion even going in late to work, something completely out of character for him. Of course, she asked him why he was getting up so late when he had always been such an early riser. "I've just been a little tired," he would respond.

That makes sense, my mom thought. After all, she was tired much of the time too, with a thirty-hour-per-week job as an attorney at a nearby law firm, a precocious two-year-old (me), and an infant to boot. Who wouldn't be tired? *And besides*, she reasoned, *Jack is eleven years older than I am; he is pretty old for a father. It can't be that easy for a man to deal with two little children at his age.*

But the changes continued. Not only did my dad begin staying up until midnight or one o'clock in the morning instead of his usual 10:00 p.m., but he started sleeping with the lights and television on. This behavior was definitely out of the ordinary because he had always required complete silence and slept in total darkness. He began waking up later and later, and every so often missed work altogether. On one occasion, he left for work in his suit and tie. When my mom called his office that afternoon to speak to him, his secretary told her that my dad had not been at work that day at all. After he got home and my mom questioned him about it, he insisted that his secretary was mistaken and that he had been at work. My mom didn't believe him. Another time, I was sick and she asked my dad to go to the nearby pharmacy to pick up a prescription for me. He didn't come back for over two hours, arriving home close to midnight. This time when my mom asked him where he had been, he just shrugged his shoulders and gave her a blank stare.

By this time my mom suspected that my dad was either having a midlife crisis or an affair. *What other explanation could there be?* she asked herself. Aside from these odd changes in his behavior, my dad seemed perfectly fine: He didn't appear to be physically ill; he was still apparently functioning satisfactorily as an attorney and managing partner at his Philadelphia law firm; and no one else seemed to notice anything unusual. She insisted that my dad accompany her to marriage counseling.

At their appointment a few weeks later, my mom brought my dad's change in behavior to the attention of the marriage counselor. My dad denied that he was having an affair and maintained that he felt fine. "I've just been a little tired and depressed," he insisted. Toward the end of the session, he complained that my brother and I had gotten into his CDs and left them all over the floor of his closet. When the counselor asked him why he didn't just clean them up, he replied, "I don't know. I just can't."

After several more sessions, the marriage counselor announced that he thought my dad might have an organic problem since the changes in his personality were so pronounced and inexplicable, and suggested that he see a neuropsychiatrist and get an MRI of his brain. My mom and dad thought this was probably unnecessary, but my dad agreed to both.

In late September, my dad underwent lengthy neuropsychological testing. In October, he reported for his MRI.

The evening after his MRI study, my dad received an urgent call from the radiologist. "I have some bad news," the radiologist said somberly. "Your MRI showed demyelination of the frontal portion of your brain consistent with cerebral adrenoleukodystrophy. You need to follow up with a neurologist who specializes in this disease as soon as possible." My dad hung up the phone and, without displaying any emotion, relayed the diagnosis to my mom.

Her heart sinking, my mom immediately began researching adrenoleukodystrophy on her computer. After several hours, she put her head down on the desk. Every article she found said the same thing: in men, the disease was invariably fatal. There was no treatment, no cure.

In that moment, my mom thought back to that day just over four years earlier, when she and my dad had vowed to spend their lives together. She drew in a painful breath and saw all of their hopes and dreams for the future unravel before her eyes. With more courage than she felt, she turned to my dad. "There has to be something we can do. We'll find a way to fight this."

"Everything will be fine," my dad replied, trying to comfort her. "Don't worry. I will be fine."

For weeks after my dad's diagnosis, my mom felt like she was living in a state of unreality. She would wake up every day with an overwhelming feeling of despair and disbelief. Her thoughts were jumbled. *How can this be happening? He doesn't look sick at all. Oh my God, all these years he's been living so frugally so he could save enough money to retire to Florida . . . it was all for nothing. What I am going to tell Taylor and Matthew? How am I possibly going to raise them myself? There has to be some kind of experimental treatment that I haven't found on the internet yet. Poor Jack. I can't believe this. I'm too young to be a widow. This can't be happening.*

She continued to take Matthew and me to daycare four days a week and went into work like nothing had changed, and yet everything had changed. What else could she do? She promised herself that no matter what happened, she would be strong for Matthew and me—no crying in front of us or allowing my dad's diagnosis to shatter our lives too.

Every day when she got home from work, she would spend her free time on the computer, scouring medical journals for some ray of hope. She compiled a list of seemingly promising experimental treatments to discuss with the specialist at the Kennedy Krieger Institute in Baltimore, where my dad had an appointment in November.

My dad remained stoic during these early weeks after his diagnosis. He took Matthew and me trick-or-treating on Halloween and continued his normal routine, attending Philadelphia Eagles games on the weekends, laughing with his friends, and talking about his plans to travel abroad in the future. "I really want to go back to Ireland," he repeatedly told my mom. The diagnosis didn't seem to faze him. My mom wondered, *How can he go on like nothing's changed? Does he truly grasp what's happening or is he in denial?* But then again, my dad had always been an unfailing optimist, always seeing the best in people and the positive side of situations.

In early November, we all piled in the car to make the three-hour journey from our home in Cherry Hill, New Jersey, to the Kennedy Krieger Institute, with my dad driving and Matthew and I strapped into our car seats in the back. My mom hadn't wanted to bring us, but she wasn't able to find a sitter that day, and the nurse at the hospital had assured her that they would arrange for someone to occupy us while she and my dad met with the doctor.

About halfway into the journey, my mom insisted that she take over the wheel; she hadn't driven with my dad in a while and was worried that he was driving much too slowly and seemed a bit distracted by the other cars. "I'm fine," my dad grumbled, but my mom was emphatic.

At Kennedy Krieger, a nurse showed Matthew and me around the hospital while my parents met with one of the hospital's renowned neurologists who had treated many patients with ALD. After scrutinizing the MRI and examining my dad, the neurologist confirmed their worst fears: there was no cure for my dad. He gently explained that my dad's cognitive and physical functioning would continue to decline, likely over the next several years, until he eventually lapsed into a vegetative state or died. The neurologist prescribed an amphetamine for my dad's fatigue, suggested that he get his affairs in order, and encouraged him to stop working and enjoy the time he had left.

It was a long car ride home, but my mom and dad acted like nothing out of the ordinary had happened so as not to alarm Matthew or me. Despite the devastating news, however, they both quietly held onto a glimmer of hope. Perhaps my dad's ALD would progress slowly and a cure would be found in time to save him—after all, neurogenetics was a rapidly evolving field. Or perhaps God would somehow spare him. Despite the bleak prognosis, they weren't going to give up without a fight.

CHAPTER THREE

Our New Normal

For the next few months, my brother and I remained blissfully unaware of my dad's diagnosis. Our daily routine went on like before. My mom dropped us off at daycare at 8:30 a.m., and then she went off to work. I don't know about my brother, but I loved daycare. All my friends were there. We did arts and crafts, played interactive games, sang songs, colored, and began to learn to read, and Ms. Nancy and Ms. Gloria were always so nice and fun to be around. My mom would invariably pick us up at 4:15 p.m., sharp. She said she didn't want us to be the last ones stuck there waiting for a ride home, and she had managed to get a job with a law firm that allowed her to work a less-than-full-time schedule, something that wasn't easy for an attorney to do, especially back then.

After daycare, we would go back home, and Matthew and I would play until dinner. My mom would try to keep us from making too much of a mess while she cleaned the house, did the laundry, and made dinner. Sometimes those late afternoons could get pretty hectic: Matthew was always getting into everything, climbing on furniture and trying to find a way to remove all of the child-proof locks, and my mom would have to stop what she was doing every few minutes to chase after him.

My dad would usually come home from work around 6:30 p.m. His sleeping patterns had improved a bit since he began taking the amphetamines the neurologist at the Kennedy Krieger Institute had prescribed for him, and it was easier for him to wake up and make it to work on time. He also felt less fatigued during the day. Sometimes he would bring my half-sister Tina over when he came home from work. We always loved when Tina came over. Tina was ten years older than me, and we didn't get to see her as much as we would have liked since she lived in Philadelphia with her mother. But on the days when Tina came over, we would all eat dinner together, and my dad would tell us funny stories and jokes. To me, our lives were perfect.

My dad had told my mom that he wanted his diagnosis to be kept a secret—from everyone—for as long as possible. He wanted our family life to continue as it always had. He also wanted to keep working despite the neurologist's suggestion that he stop. "Working is such a big part of my life," he told my mom. "I have so many clients depending on me. I can't just quit. I worked so hard to get where I am now."

My mom quietly feared that soon, though, hers might be the only income. She began to make plans to increase her hours at work. *What's going to happen when his illness progresses and we don't have his salary to rely on anymore?* she asked herself. *Although I'd love to be able to work fewer hours right now, I have to be realistic. If Jack dies, I'm going to have to support Taylor and Matthew by myself. We're going to need health insurance.* She began looking for a nanny.

By January 2002, less than two months later, my dad's sleeping problems had returned. It seemed as though the amphetamines were no longer working: Once again he was having a hard time getting up in the morning and was staying up late at night. To compound matters, he was having a great deal of difficulty walking. He complained that his legs felt weak and numb, and at times he couldn't maintain his balance. While my dad had had minor stability issues and a somewhat abnormal gait since his mid-twenties (this was originally diagnosed as a common foot condition for which he had to wear orthotics, but was ultimately determined to be adrenomyeloneuropathy, a less serious variant of ALD), he had never had any problems getting out of a chair or climbing up and down the stairs like he did now.

Soon more alarming problems began to emerge. Even more distressing to my mom than the fact that my dad was sporadically unable to control his bladder and bowels was the fact that he didn't seem to notice. Or care. "Jack," she would exclaim sharply, "the couch is soaked where you were sitting." Or, "Look at the front of your pants—you can't go out of the house like that!" On these occasions, my dad would simply shrug and walk away. He seemed oblivious to the fact that his pants were stained or smelled like urine. Every once in a while, he would urinate on the floor in front of the toilet and just walk out of the bathroom without cleaning it up. *Oh my God*, my mom thought, *he was always so obsessive about cleanliness and personal hygiene—he wouldn't even burp Matthew without a huge towel draped over his entire body. He must have some strange form of ALD-related dementia—yet, he's still working, driving, and seemingly functioning fine outside the house. Am I the only one who's noticed that something's wrong?*

My dad also became increasingly reluctant to shower, shave, or brush his teeth on a regular basis. "Jack, please," my mom would plead with him, "you need to shower!" Or, "For goodness' sake, brush your teeth!" My dad would simply reply, "I don't feel like it," or give her a blank stare. Sometimes he would try to convince her she was mistaken and that he actually had showered and shaved. But it was often clear that he hadn't.

Occasionally at night, my dad would engage in a strange ritual of removing his shirt and slapping his stomach with both hands. He would do this over and over for hours, to the point where his stomach had bright red hand marks on it. Whenever he did this, he would repeatedly sing the Lynyrd Skynyrd song "Sweet Home Alabama," varying the pitch of his voice with each stanza. Although Matthew and I thought he was trying to be funny and often sang along with him, it unnerved my mom. "Stop singing that song!" she would holler at all of us. "I can't take it!"

Still, aside from the times my dad exhibited these strange behaviors, he seemed completely normal. He also had an uncanny ability to snap out of these "spells," as my mom called them, when other people were around or when he was outside of the house.

In late January, however, my mom insisted that they break the news of his diagnosis to close friends and family, just in case they had noticed his unusual behavior or would in the future, when his symptoms would undoubtedly get worse. My dad reluctantly agreed.

Telling people wasn't easy. They told their friends and my mom's family first. My mom calmly explained over and over that my dad had been diagnosed with a rare genetic disease called adrenoleukodystrophy and that, according to the doctors, the prognosis wasn't good: He would likely deteriorate both physically and mentally over the next few years and was not expected to survive much longer than that.

Not surprisingly, everyone they told was both shocked and devastated by the news—no one had suspected a thing, and my dad was a man in the prime of his life with young children to raise. My mom also informed them that since ALD was an X-linked genetic disorder, I was by default a carrier of the disease, but that the doctors had assured her that female carriers do not get symptoms, so at least there was no need to be concerned about me. She reassured everyone that she and my dad were fine at least for the time being, and that they were exploring every possible treatment, hoping for some sort of miracle.

Telling my dad's family was much more difficult; after all, given the pattern of inheritance of X-linked diseases, it was clear that in addition to the fact that my dad inherited the disease from his mother, both of his brothers could have inherited the defective gene and might eventually suffer the same fate as my dad. My dad's sister Patty, my parents had also concluded, was also most likely a carrier of the disease, as her own son had died suddenly of adrenal insufficiency as a young adult, which they now knew was a hallmark symptom of ALD. When my dad broke the news to his family, however, his parents and sister seemed skeptical of the diagnosis and prognosis, proclaiming that they saw him at least twice a week and that he seemed perfectly fine and that no such disease ran in their family. *They must be in denial*, my mom thought. *Or perhaps, they don't really understand. After all, Jack's parents are both approaching eighty, and Patty must be nearly sixty. Maybe they just can't face the fact that Jack is sick.* My mom didn't know for sure, but either way, she found their reaction baffling.

A few days later, my dad asked my mom to meet with his priest to discuss the Catholic faith's views on end-of-life issues, such as the implementation and withdrawal of artificial life support. He had already decided, he told the priest, that as long as it wasn't contrary to his Catholic faith, he wanted to be kept alive for as long as possible by whatever means necessary, regardless of his condition or the cost. The priest told him that this would pose no religious concerns, but my mom looked at my dad with surprise. "Are you sure, Jack?" she asked him. "What if your disease progresses to the point where the doctors think you'll be physically and mentally incapacitated or on a respirator for the rest of your life?"

"I still want to be kept alive," my dad insisted, "no matter what."

My mom shook her head, not completely sure whether he fully comprehended the magnitude of such a decision. Later, doctors would tell her that when my dad had made this statement, his decision-making capacity was obviously impaired and he could not have meant what he said. But my mom knew in her heart that he did. You see, my dad loved life. He had always lived every day to the fullest. He lived with passion and joy and enthusiasm and curiosity and understanding and humor. My mom knew that it wasn't that my dad was afraid to die: He had his faith and never questioned his deep-rooted belief that he would ultimately be going to a better place. It was just that he didn't want to leave us—not yet, not anytime soon. And it was also because he had an unshakeable conviction that someday, somehow, there would be a cure.

CHAPTER FOUR

The Magic Kingdom

When my mom told me we were going to Disney World that February, I couldn't contain my excitement. We had been to Disney several years earlier, when I was two, but I had spent most of my time fixated on Minnie Mouse then. Now I was fascinated by Cinderella, Ariel, and Belle, and had my heart set on being a princess when I grew up.

"Matthew was just a baby last time we were there," my mom reminded me. "He should be old enough to enjoy it this time."

The neurologist had told my dad back in November that if he wanted to travel, he should do so as soon as possible, and my mom had been planning this trip ever since. My parents had both rearranged their work schedules to take five days off in a row. At first my mom had planned for us to go to Turks and Caicos, since she and my dad had always wanted to go there, but they decided Disney World would be a better choice since it was closer to home and my dad would probably have a hard time walking on a sandy beach. My mom knew that this might be our last family vacation together, and she was determined to make it a memorable one—one that we all would enjoy.

When the morning we were to leave for Disney finally came, my mom had a hard time getting my dad out of bed.

"I'm so tired. Just give me a few more minutes," he kept repeating.

Matthew and I jumped on his bed to try to hurry him up, but he just kept laying there with his eyes closed.

"Come on, Daddy," I cried, "it's time to go. We're all ready but you. Mommy says we have to leave now or we'll miss the plane."

Finally, my dad got up and slowly got dressed. We made it to the airport and onto the plane without a minute to spare. My mom sat in between Matthew and me, and my dad sat across the aisle, as we took off on our three-hour flight to Orlando.

After an uneventful flight and a short drive in our rental car, we made it to our hotel. We were finally at Disney! My mom unpacked our suitcases and, since it was almost dinner time, we went to Chef Mickey's restaurant, which was on the bottom floor of our hotel.

I couldn't get over Chef Mickey's. It was amazing—like a dream come true—with its bright lights and bold colors and Disney character decor. Matthew and I were both so excited, especially when Goofy came over to our table and posed for pictures with us. "This vacation is going to be so great!" I exclaimed.

As we were finishing dinner, my mom said she had to run up to the room to change Matthew's diaper, and that she would be back in a few minutes. She told my dad to keep a close eye on me, as I was known to wander. Soon after they left the restaurant, Mickey Mouse appeared, and I just knew I had to meet him! He was instantly surrounded by other children.

"Daddy!" I cried. "I'm going to go talk to Mickey!" I ran over to Mickey and stood in line behind the other children waiting to meet him. After what seemed like an eternity, it was finally my turn. I told Mickey my name and he wrapped his arms around me in a big hug. I wanted my dad to take a picture, but I didn't see him.

After my time with Mickey was up, I turned to look for my dad. I still didn't see him anywhere, not even at the table where we had eaten dinner. I walked around Chef Mickey's looking for him, but I couldn't find him. I figured he would be back soon, and I didn't know what to do or how to find my mom and Matthew, so I got back in line to see Mickey again.

Suddenly, a woman tapped on my shoulder and asked if I was lost. I told her I wasn't lost; I just couldn't find my dad. She helped me look around the restaurant and then asked me my name so she could try to find my mom. The woman was able to locate our room number and called my mom on the hotel phone.

"I have Taylor with me," she told my mom. "She's down here at Chef Mickey's—alone."

My mom told that her dad should have been with me, and she hurried back down to the restaurant with Matthew.

"Taylor, where did your dad go?" she nervously asked me.

"He was sitting at the table when I went to see Mickey Mouse. I don't know where he went. I looked everywhere for him."

My mom thanked the woman for calling her, and we continued searching for my dad. He was nowhere to be found. After an hour or so, my mom gave up and we all went back up to the room. She figured he couldn't have made it very far, and he always seemed to be disappearing lately.

After she put Matthew and me to bed and my dad still hadn't come back, she worriedly paced the room. *What do I do?* she frantically asked herself. *I can't go out to look for him and leave the kids here alone. Where could he be? Maybe he fell in a bathroom or something. Should I call someone? Damn, I really wish I would have listened to him when he said we should both get cell phones.*

At around 12:15 a.m., there was a knock on the door. When my mom answered it, a hotel supervisor was standing outside with my dad. The supervisor told her that he had noticed my dad sitting on a chair outside Chef Mickey's and that he seemed a bit disoriented. The supervisor said that my dad seemed a little wobbly when he tried to stand up, so he offered to walk him to our room. My mom realized that the man thought my dad was drunk.

"How could you leave Taylor by herself?" my mom pointedly asked my dad after she shut the door. "She could have been kidnapped! I told you I would be back down in a few minutes. Where have you been all night?"

My dad gave her a dazed look. "Sitting around on benches." My mom had a sinking feeling that my dad's condition was far worse than she had realized.

The next morning Matthew and I woke up eager to take the monorail into the Magic Kingdom, but my dad wouldn't get out of bed. My mom put on the television and we watched cartoons for a few hours, repeatedly asking her when we could go to the rides. By lunchtime, my mom had finally managed to pull my dad into a sitting position on the bed, but my dad said was that his legs were completely numb. He tried to get up, but he couldn't walk at all, not even with my mom holding him up.

How could he have gotten so much worse this fast? my mom wondered. *Maybe it's being in a different environment? Or maybe I've just been so busy working and taking care of the kids I didn't notice how sick he really was?* She called the front desk to see if she could get a wheelchair for my dad but was told that all of the wheelchairs had already been rented. *This vacation was a big mistake*, she thought.

"Just take the kids to the park," my dad insisted. "I'm alright. I'm just tired and my legs are weak. I want to stay in bed for a few hours."

My mom was afraid to leave him, but she also didn't want to disappoint Matthew and me and ruin our vacation. She made my dad promise to stay in bed and told him we'd be back in a few hours. So, we went to the Magic Kingdom without him.

We had fun, but my mom was worried about my dad the whole time, and we returned to the room far sooner than Matthew and I would have liked. Fortunately, my dad was still there when we got back, sitting up in bed and staring into space, slapping his stomach over and over.

The next day, my dad was able to walk a little bit, and my mom was able to arrange for him to get a motorized scooter so we could all go to the Magic Kingdom together. Once we got to the park, however, my dad didn't seem very enthusiastic and had a lot of difficulty operating the scooter. Despite our repeated begging, my mom wouldn't let Matthew or me ride on the scooter with him because he kept running into trash cans and other roadblocks around the park. Sometimes he would get stuck in a tight spot and couldn't navigate out without my mom's help. But there was a benefit to the scooter—we were able to skip the long lines for some of the rides by using a special entrance reserved for people who were disabled. We got to go on some amazing rides, like It's a Small World and Pirates of the Caribbean, and we even watched the Disney parade! Matthew and I were having the time of our lives, but not so much my dad, who seemed to be in a daze for much of the day.

The next few days progressed in a similar fashion, with Matthew and I enjoying Disney, my dad using his scooter and appearing to be out of it much of the time, and my mom growing increasingly frantic at how quickly she felt my dad's mental state was deteriorating. She would plead with him to shower and change his clothes every night. Though my dad was very quiet most of the time and rarely said anything to my mom or Matthew and me, somehow he was still able to talk on the phone like nothing was wrong. He called his office every day to check on work and reported to his secretary and the attorneys at his office that we were all having a fantastic time—that we were all up bright and early every day and that he was getting a lot of exercise from all the walking around we were doing.

The day before our vacation was due to end, Matthew came down with a twenty-four-hour stomach bug. He was throwing up everywhere—all over our hotel room floor and on the bed. It was horrible and seemed like it would never stop. My mom had to keep calling room service for more towels to clean up after him, and she tried to keep him from running around the room screaming. My dad just sat in his chair and watched the pile of soiled towels grow higher and higher, slapping his stomach and singing "Sweet Home Alabama." *Oh my God, I literally can't take this anymore*, my mom thought in desperation, *we have to get home—but how? I can't take Matthew on a plane in his condition, not to mention the fact that I'm not sure I can even get Jack through the airport since he can barely walk. And how will I manage all of this luggage with the three of them?* She decided that she would put us all in the rental car (with a few towels for Matthew) and drive the eighteen hours it would take to get home.

It ended up taking us two full days to get back to New Jersey. Matthew was no longer sick, thank goodness, but my dad asked my mom to stop every hour or so at rest stops so he could use a restroom. Getting him from the car to the restrooms was no easy chore, though, and sometimes it would take her a half hour just to help him stand up from his seat and walk there. Sometimes he would stay in the men's room for so long she would have to call in to make sure he was okay, while we were all waiting for him outside the door.

We stopped halfway through our road trip and stayed overnight in a somewhat squalid hotel in North Carolina so we could get some sleep. The next day, we finally made it home.

From my perspective as a three-and-a-half-year-old, our vacation to Disney was all that I could have hoped for, and any bumps in the road were just a small part of a grand and magical adventure. While I understood that my dad was acting strange and was having problems walking, I still didn't and couldn't comprehend the extent of his illness, nor did it dampen my youthful enthusiasm. To me, our family vacation couldn't have been better. My mom later told me it was one of the worst experiences of her life.

CHAPTER FIVE

Running Away

One of the first things that my parents did when we got back from Disney was to try to find a neurologist in the Philadelphia/South Jersey area with experience treating ALD who could see my dad on a regular basis, since it wasn't feasible for them to keep traveling back and forth to the Kennedy Krieger Institute. Due to the rarity of the disease, finding a doctor familiar with ALD wasn't easy, so they settled for a well-respected neurologist at Pennsylvania Hospital who specialized in treating patients with ALS, also known as Lou Gehrig's disease. Although ALD and ALS are both neurodegenerative disorders that have some overlapping symptoms, they are two very different diseases. But the neurologist agreed to consult with the neurologist at the Kennedy Krieger Institute, and my dad held him in high regard. My mom also arranged for one of her friend's fathers who was a prominent local neuropsychiatrist to begin seeing my dad.

My mom had been keeping a detailed diary of my dad's unusual behavior and physical symptoms, and informed the doctors of his seemingly rapid deterioration during our vacation. My dad, who was now able to walk again, albeit with a cane, listened to my mom's description but insisted that he was "just a little tired" and still holding down his job as an attorney with no problem whatsoever.

"Nobody but me seems to notice that there is anything wrong," she told the doctors. "When he's home, he barely speaks and tells me he has a 'mental block' that prevents him from showering and shaving. He also engages in these strange ritualistic behaviors, sometimes for hours on end. But then he has this remarkable ability to act perfectly normal in front of other people, and when he speaks on the telephone he sounds so articulate, I wonder if it's me who's going crazy."

The doctors assured my mom privately that it was not her imagination, that patients with certain types of brain degeneration can function quite well in public, and that their symptoms became much more pronounced when they let their guard down. They also mentioned that it was not unheard of for a person with his condition to be much more conversant when speaking into a telephone or microphone, as the placement of such objects close to the mouth somehow activates the area of the brain responsible for speech.

"There have been times when he went into work after not showering for days. A few times he even left the house wearing urine-stained suit pants which he refused to change," my mom explained with despair. "When I begged him to bathe and change his clothes, he wouldn't listen to me. I even tried to physically restrain him from leaving the house so he wouldn't embarrass himself at work, but he just pushed me aside and left anyway. Is there anything I can do when this happens?"

There was no easy answer. My dad, the doctors said, was clearly in the early stages of dementia as a result of the deterioration of the frontal lobe of his brain.

Before we left for Disney, my mom had hired a nanny to come to our house every afternoon so my mom could stay later at work. Matthew and I fell in love with Paula the first time we met her. She was my mom's age and had three children of her own. We began going to daycare in the mornings only, and Paula would pick us up after lunch and bring us home. She loved to cuddle with us on the sofa and would take us to the playground or play games with us. Paula and my mom became fast friends, and soon she was like a member of our family.

Not long after Paula started working for us, my dad's partners informed him that they had voted him out of his law firm. His career was officially over. My dad was completely and utterly devastated. He had worked at the same firm ever since he had graduated from law school and had quickly risen up the ranks to become a managing partner as a result of his excellent people skills and negotiation prowess. He had loved representing working-class men and women whom he believed needed a helping hand, and he was a favorite among the firm's clients. He tried to negotiate with his partners for a part-time position or one where he could work from home, but to no avail. They wouldn't have it.

My mom wasn't surprised, but her heart ached for my dad because he was so upset. She was also angry because she felt his termination had been handled callously; after all, my dad had poured his heart and soul into that law firm for almost thirty years, and the only thing he was guilty of was getting sick. *There was no need to treat him like a leper*, she silently raged. My dad, of course, didn't hold any grudges—he had never been that kind of person—he just asked my mom over and over, "What am I going to do all day now?" Every time she tried to console him, he would tell her, "I need to work. I know I can still do it. If it wasn't for the weakness in my legs, this never would have happened."

But my mom knew it was much more than that. *Well, at least he can still talk on the phone*, she thought. *Maybe I can find him some sort of part-time job as a telephone solicitor or something else in sales where he can work from home.*

A few days later, though, before she had time to even begin scouring the help-wanted ads, she came home from work to an unwelcome surprise: a notice stating that our electricity was about to be shut off due to an unpaid bill. "Jack," she asked, "haven't you been paying the electric bill?"

"Yeah, I think so," my dad replied in a weak voice.

"This notification says the bill hasn't been paid in two months and that we owe over seven hundred dollars."

My dad shrugged.

"So is this notice right? Do you have your checkbook register so we can check to see when you last paid the bill?"

My dad found his checkbook in his desk drawer and handed it to her.

My mom scanned the register then looked at my dad in dismay. "According to your checkbook, you haven't paid any bills since January. Did you not record the checks you wrote, or did you just not pay the bills?"

"I don't know."

My mom checked his desk drawer and found a tall stack of unopened bills. *This is just great,* she chastised herself, *I should have thought to double check to make sure he was paying the bills. We probably owe hundreds of dollars in interest fees and late charges on top of all these unpaid bills. It's going to take me days to sort all this out.*

"Don't worry, I'll go through all of these later tonight after the kids are asleep and see if I can figure out what we owe," she told my dad. "But right now I have a million things to do, and I still have to make dinner."

When we sat down to eat that night, my dad still seemed upset. "I told you not to worry about the bills," my mom said gently. "I'll figure out what needs to be paid and write out checks for you to sign. We're going to have to pay the bills out of your account, though, because I just paid my share of the bills out of my account last week, and I'm not getting a paycheck again until next Friday. I hope you have enough money in the bank."

"That's not it," my dad said. "It's . . . well . . . " He pointed to his throat. "It's been hard for me to swallow lately, even water."

My mom looked at him with concern. "Your voice sounds a little raspy. Maybe it's just a cold coming on, or allergies? Do you want me to cut up your steak in smaller pieces? Will that help?"

"No," my dad shook his head. But he went to bed that night without eating any dinner.

Over the next few weeks, my mom managed to get a great deal accomplished. She took over the responsibility for paying all of the household bills, helped my dad apply for social security disability benefits and for continuation of his health insurance benefits, and fought with the insurance company to get him a hospital bed since it was becoming increasingly difficult for him to sit up from a lying down position or get out of bed on his own. She also arranged for my dad to get in-home physical therapy and to be evaluated by a specialist in swallowing disorders.

Since my mom was afraid to leave my dad alone while she was at work, Paula began coming to our house full time. Matthew and I still went to daycare several mornings a week, even though Paula was home with my dad, as my mom had always felt that it was beneficial for us to be in a structured environment with other children our age, and she was willing to pay the extra cost to make sure that happened.

By now, I was old enough to understand that my dad was very sick with a disease called ALD. I would often lie beside him in his hospital bed upstairs, in what used to be Matthew's room, watching my favorite cartoons. My dad seemed to like watching them too, even *Powerpuff Girls*. I would talk to him about everything, and although he didn't always respond, I could tell he loved my company. At the same time, I missed my mom. She always seemed to be busy now; she was working longer hours, and at night she was focused on bills and insurance policies and paperwork involving my dad.

One day, my mom came home from work early. I thought that maybe she was going to take me somewhere fun, but no—she and one of my dad's friends were sitting in on my dad's appointment with the swallowing specialist. I'm not sure what came over me, but I decided that I wanted out. I convinced Matthew that we should run away from home. Back then, he agreed with whatever I said—I was his older sister, after all—so we put some clothes in my pink Barbie suitcase and slipped out the porch window while my mom was busy in the other room. We quickly ran down the sidewalk as we made our getaway, and then began walking when our house was no longer visible.

We were probably a half mile or so away from home when a police car drove past us and then stopped. A police officer got out of the car and asked

Matthew and me where we were going. "Running away!" I told him. That did not go over well. He told us to get in the back of the car and said that he would be taking us home. I reluctantly gave him our address. The officer didn't talk to us at all on the ride home, and he seemed pretty angry. Matthew and I were both scared. I clutched my Barbie suitcase.

When we got to our house, the officer told us to walk next to him up to the door. When my mom answered, I could tell that she was confused and that she hadn't even noticed that we had been gone.

"Ma'am, are these your children?"

"Yes. Where did . . . I guess they must have slipped out of the house somehow."

"Well, that's obviously a serious problem, ma'am. They were several blocks away when I spotted them." He peered into the house and saw my dad, his friend, and the swallowing specialist sitting in the living room. "So there are four adults in this house and no one was supervising these children?"

"Officer, you don't understand," my mom tried to explain. "My husband is . . . well, he's sick, and I was just having him evaluated by a specialist . . . and I thought the kids were on the porch. There aren't any doors to the outside, and all of the windows were shut. I don't know how they got outside."

I could see the apprehension in her eyes as the officer sternly lectured her, using phrases like "inadequate supervision" and "negligence." I was sure my mom was going to be arrested. I think she thought so too. My dad's friend, who was also an attorney, came over and privately spoke to the police officer outside the front door. When they came back, the police officer warned my mom that she better be more careful and that there better not be a next time. At long last, he turned to go back to his car.

"Taylor, what were you thinking! How could you just leave the house like that—and to drag your brother with you!" she scolded me after the officer left. "I can't turn my back for five minutes to help your father without something like this happening . . . do you know how much trouble you could have caused?"

"I'm sorry," I told her with tears in my eyes. I was truly upset and ashamed for trying to run away from home. To this day, I'm not sure why I did it. I guess it must have been my way of trying to get my mom's attention, since it always seemed like she was busy working or taking care of my dad.

Looking back on it now, I'm sure my mom must have wanted to run away sometimes too.

CHAPTER SIX

Firemen and Fundraisers

Throughout the spring of 2002, my dad's condition continued to decline. Neither the therapy for his legs nor his swallowing difficulty seemed to be working very well. He started choking on food when he ate and was losing weight as a result. He also began to fall a lot, especially at night when he was tired. Whenever he fell, my mom had a hard time getting him back up because his legs were too weak to offer any assistance.

One night at around eleven o'clock, when my dad was coming downstairs, he tripped on a step and slid down to the first floor landing. He wasn't hurt, but he couldn't get up, not even with my mom's help. She struggled to lift him for an hour or so, taking breaks to try to allow him to regain some of the strength he had left in his legs, but she just couldn't budge him. Matthew and I had still been awake in our bedrooms when my dad fell, and we ran downstairs to see him stuck, half-sitting, half-lying at the bottom of the steps. My mom thought it was too late to call any friends or family members, so she dialed 911 for help. She was told that she needed to call the fire department.

A fire truck was dispatched to our house, and three firemen came in and surrounded my dad at the bottom of the stairway. They lifted him up easily and carried him back upstairs to his hospital bed. The firemen were so funny and nice to Matthew and me, and they gave us each plastic purple gloves like the ones they were wearing when they helped my dad. We were very excited to have actual firemen in our house, and after they left Matthew and I put both sets of gloves in a small box in my bedroom closet. For the next year or so, every so often we would take the plastic purple gloves out of that box and wear them and pretend we were saving my dad.

After the night the firemen came, my mom begged my dad not to try to go down the stairs anymore without someone there to help. "When you want to go downstairs, just let me know, and if I'm not home, call for Paula," she implored him. She considered having his hospital bed moved downstairs so he wouldn't have to use the steps, but decided against it because she didn't want him sleeping on a different floor than the rest of us.

Despite the exacerbation of my dad's physical symptoms that spring, he still repeatedly insisted that he was bored sitting home and wanted to work. My mom finally found the time to look into finding him some kind of part-time job or volunteer opportunity, but she couldn't come up with anything that was feasible. After all, the doctors had told my dad that he shouldn't drive, and even on the days he was able to walk with a cane or a walker, it was so difficult for him to get dressed, much less get out of the house. Plus, my mom didn't know how she could manage transporting him anywhere on a regular basis; there was already so much chaos in our house in the mornings, it was hard enough for her to get out of the house herself and make it to her own job on time. But then she had an idea.

"Hey, Jack, why don't we put together some kind of fundraiser to raise awareness of ALD and benefit ALD research? Maybe we could hold a charity dinner or organize a walk or something like that. We could get a list together of the phone numbers of all of your friends and business connections, and you could call them and invite them to the event, or at least try to get them to donate. It would be like a job for you. And it could help so many people."

My dad loved the idea.

So my mom got to work. After she had researched various options, they decided to organize a 5k run. My mom particularly liked this idea because she had always loved to run herself. When Matthew and I were younger, she used to jog around the neighborhood or run in races while my dad stayed home and watched us. But of course that all ended once he got sick. Now she couldn't leave the house—not even for five minutes—without hiring a sitter or asking someone to come over and stay with us. And since she hated imposing on people, especially when it wasn't for something she considered to be really important, she didn't run anymore.

My mom managed to find a race director who had worked with a number of nonprofit organizations, and she and my dad decided to hold the event in a local park that contained a popular 5k course. My mom knew that in order to get corporate sponsors, they would have to form a legitimate nonprofit organization. She filed the necessary paperwork with the IRS and asked my dad's cousin and some friends to join the board of directors. It wasn't long before "Run for ALD" was born.

My mom convened the first of the monthly meetings of the board of directors around our kitchen table soon after filing the paperwork. The board decided that all of the money raised from the event would be donated to the Kennedy Krieger Institute and earmarked for ALD research. The date for the 5k run was set for September 8, 2002. There was a lot to do in a short time, and each of the board members volunteered to take on a significant assignment.

My dad's job was to secure sponsors for the event. My mom gave him a long list of telephone numbers as promised. For the next few weeks while she was at work, he kept himself busy calling friends and business acquaintances, telling them about the fundraiser and asking them to sponsor and/or participate in the Run for ALD. Many of the people my dad called were unaware of his diagnosis and were more than happy to contribute to the cause. Despite my dad's deteriorating condition, he had no difficulty talking on the phone and reveled in his new role as a fundraiser. And when the checks began rolling in, my dad was happier than he had been in a very long time, knowing that once again he was able to do something to help other people.

CHAPTER SEVEN

Making Mountains Out of Molehills

While having my dad make fundraising phone calls was proving to be very successful as far as the Run for ALD was concerned, it did have some major drawbacks. For one, he began ordering lavish items over the phone, usually things he saw on infomercials. Most of the things he ordered were not only completely unnecessary, but extremely expensive.

One day when my mom came home from work, several massive boxes containing a pricey home gym were laying on the floor inside the front door. The boxes were so heavy my mom couldn't move them. My dad acknowledged ordering the gym on his credit card and told her he was planning to begin working out.

"But Jack," she exclaimed, "you can barely get out of bed. How could you ever use a home gym? We have to return it."

But the manufacturer refused to pick up the gym, even after my mom tried to explain that my dad was sick and didn't understand what he was doing when he ordered it. "The item isn't defective," they insisted, "and your husband provided his credit card number over the phone."

Other items began to arrive in quick succession—vacuums and encyclopedias and pasta makers and jewelry—and more things he could never or would never use. Although my mom felt terribly guilty, she canceled all of my dad's credit cards.

That still didn't solve the problem, however. A few weeks later, a bill arrived indicating that my dad had purchased a timeshare that had cost thousands of dollars. My mom immediately got on the phone and informed the seller that not only did my dad have a brain disorder, but he didn't have any credit cards, and insisted that they cancel his order. The seller refused, advising her that they had given my dad "instant credit" based on his salary as an attorney.

"His salary as an attorney? He's sick—he doesn't even work anymore! How could you have given him instant credit over the phone?" She finally managed to convince the seller to cancel the timeshare, but not without having to threaten legal action if they refused to do so. She instructed Paula that she would have to begin watching my dad like a hawk and monitoring his phone conversations. This didn't prove to be easy, though, as my dad usually stayed upstairs in his room, and Paula couldn't devote all of her time to watching him. So every so often, more unwanted items would show up at the house.

In addition to his obsession with ordering infomercial items, my dad would repeatedly phone my mom when she was at work—sometimes every five minutes—to inform her that there were moles in his bedroom. He was absolutely convinced of this, and insisted that there were two moles that appeared in his room several times a day and ran along the railings of his hospital bed and across the carpet. My mom and Paula thought that it was possible that there were mice in his room or that some other type of rodent could have gotten into the house. We all searched for the moles for weeks—even Matthew and me—but we never found anything. Although my mom repeatedly assured me my dad must have been imagining the moles, I was haunted by the thought that there could be some kind of gnawing mammals running around our house. A few times I woke up screaming after having nightmares that there were huge moles crawling on my bed.

Aside from these issues, after working to secure sponsors for the Run for ALD for several weeks, my dad seemed to have a newfound energy. He became more communicative and miraculously regained his ability to walk relatively well using his cane. The doctors couldn't explain it, but there he was, pacing around the house, itching to get out.

My mom would take us all to various places, like to the park and to Target (he always wanted to go to Target), but he still wasn't satisfied. He insisted that he wanted to go out by himself and repeatedly asked my mom to leave him his car keys when she went to work. My mom would remind him that the doctors had said he wasn't allowed to drive (she had hidden his car keys so he couldn't find them), but he insisted this wasn't true and that he could drive just fine. He started to become extremely agitated every time he wanted to leave the house but couldn't find his car keys, and would sometimes spend the entire day when my mom was at work searching for them. He looked through drawers and on shelves, in coat pockets and in every nook and cranny he could find. He kept begging Paula to give him the keys and tried to convince her that my mom and the doctors were in a conspiracy against him to try to destroy his life by keeping him confined to the house.

One day when my mom was at work, she received a call from Paula.

"Jack's gone," Paula said in a nervous voice. "I looked in the driveway and his car is gone too. He must have found an extra set of keys somewhere. I was in the basement with Matthew and I didn't even hear him leave. What should I do?"

"I'll leave right now. I'll be home in a few minutes. Hopefully, I'll pass him on the way."

But my dad still wasn't back by the time she got home. "I think I better call the police," my mom told Paula. "He hasn't driven for months, and I don't trust him behind the wheel at all. He gets distracted so easily, and he's obviously delusional, at least some of the time. What if he crashes and hurts himself or someone else?"

Fifteen minutes later, a police officer came to the door. My mom let him in and she explained the situation. "His driver's license hasn't technically been revoked or anything," she clarified, "but he has a rare genetic disease that is causing his brain to deteriorate. He sees moles in his room. If you need some kind of proof, I have medical reports that say he has dementia. The doctors said he shouldn't drive."

The officer told her to remain calm and asked for a description of my dad and the car he was driving. He made a call and informed my mom and Paula that they were putting an APB out on my dad.

I didn't know what an APB was, but I was scared. "Is my dad going to be put in jail?" I asked the officer.

"No," he stated kindly. "Don't worry," he told my mom, as he was leaving. "We'll call you as soon as we find him."

We all waited in the living room, worrying about my dad. The time seemed to drag on forever. An hour and a half went by—still no word. Paula felt bad that my dad had escaped with the car during her watch, but my mom assured her that it wasn't her fault. "You can't have eyes in the back of your head," she empathized. "Believe me, I know how hard it is to watch them all."

Suddenly, we heard a noise at the front door, and my dad came staggering in.

"Jack!" my mom cried with relief, "where have you been? You know you're not supposed to drive!"

"What's the big deal?" he mumbled. "I just went to the Dollar Store."

"Well, we called the police! You could have been in an accident!"

My dad shrugged his shoulders and walked back outside to his car. We followed him out and watched him open his trunk. Inside the trunk were dozens upon dozens of Dollar Store items. There were little bottles of shampoo, candle holders, plastic picture frames, greeting cards, bags of colorful balloons, potholders, coin wrappers, and at least twenty fly swatters. No one spoke. My mom knew there was no point in asking him why.

"Did you at least pay for this stuff?" she asked my dad. He handed her a receipt.

The police officer that we had talked to earlier pulled up behind my dad's car in the driveway as we continued to survey the array of items inside his trunk.

"He came back himself," my mom told the officer. "He was apparently at the Dollar Store a few miles down the road."

"She's in a conspiracy with my doctors," my dad tried to explain. "I can drive."

The officer peered inside the trunk, then looked at my mom with compassion.

"He has a receipt," my mom assured him. "I'll make sure he doesn't get the keys again."

After dinner that night, my mom and I sat at the kitchen table with all the stuff my dad had bought spread out in front of us. For a while, I wasn't sure if she was going to laugh or cry. Then she stood up and went over to the refrigerator and took out two bottles of beer—one for my dad, who was sitting in the family room with Matthew, and one for herself. "I actually hate beer," she said, but proceeded to drink it anyway. She blew up a few of the Dollar Store balloons, pulled me into the family room, and handed each of us a fly swatter. We spent the next hour or so swatting the balloons back and forth between us, trying to prevent them from hitting the ground. My dad played from the sofa, and my mom from a chair, while Matthew and I ran around the room laughing and chasing the balloons with our fly swatters.

That night, at least for a little while, it seemed like everything had gone back to normal. Just like it was before my dad got sick. But from this time on, our lives would continue to get more confusing, more complicated, and more . . . well, rare.

CHAPTER EIGHT

When It Rains, It Pours

Within a matter of a few weeks, my dad's ability to walk deteriorated again as quickly as it had improved. He began to have so much difficulty walking, in fact, that he rarely got out of his hospital bed, instead lying there all day and watching television. One morning before my mom left for work, however, he told her that he, too, was going into work. He sat up on the edge of his bed and tried to lace his work shoes. My mom tried to get him to lie back down and reminded him that he didn't work anymore. He wouldn't listen and insisted he was going into his office.

Eight hours later, when my mom got home, she went upstairs and found my dad still sitting on the edge of the bed—still trying to tie his shoes and go to work. My mom later told me this was one of the saddest sights she had even seen, and that it brought tears to her eyes every time she thought about it. "Your father loved his job so much," she explained, "I think it was just impossible for him to accept the fact that he couldn't work anymore. He never seemed to understand that anything was wrong with him besides his problems walking."

When my dad did get out of bed that spring, it was usually to use the bathroom, and my mom or Paula would have to help him get there with the aid of a walker. Sometimes he would stay in the bathroom for so long they would worry that something had happened and would have go in to get him out. A few times, for some reason they did not quite understand, the toilet or the sink would overflow when he was in there by himself, and water would come seeping out under the door into the hallway.

One night, when my mom was nearly at her wits' end between working full time and taking care of all of us—not to mention fighting with the insurance company over my dad's medical bills, trying to handle his social security and long-term disability claims, returning the various items he had ordered, searching for moles, and planning the upcoming Run for ALD—the ceiling in our family room suddenly caved in, and water began pouring through the hole that had formed over our heads. My mom ran upstairs to the bathroom and found my dad standing inside watching the sink and the toilet overflowing, with nearly four inches of water on the floor around him. She got my dad out of the bathroom and began sobbing as she ran around the house gathering up all of the towels she could find to try to soak up the water. Matthew and I were frightened by my mom's emotional outburst since she was usually quite stoic, and we grabbed towels from our bathroom closet to try to help her mop up the bathroom floor.

"Just take the towels downstairs and put them on the carpet where the water's coming through the ceiling," she pleaded. "Be careful and don't stand anywhere near the hole in the ceiling. I'll be down in a few minutes."

Matthew and I ran back downstairs with our towels. Water was still pouring through the ceiling so hard it looked like it was raining. We put the towels down to catch the water, and then I had an idea. I got my mom's umbrella out of our hallway closet and opened it up (even though I knew we weren't supposed to open umbrellas in the house). When my mom came back downstairs, Matthew and I were both standing under the umbrella directly under the ceiling where the water was coming through. I thought it was funny, but my mom didn't laugh. She didn't yell at us either, though. She just collapsed on the sofa and put her head in her hands. Then, after a few minutes, she picked up the phone.

"Hi, Carole, it's Diane. I realize I said no to your suggestion that Sam come to live in our house for a while, but I've changed my mind. I really do need help. Can you have him call me to can see if we can work something out?"

Carole was one of my mom's best friends. She had recently separated from her husband, Sam, and was extremely worried because Sam had lost his job, then his car, and was in the process of getting evicted from their apartment. Suffice it to say he was more than a little depressed and in desperate need of a place to live. Carole had implored my mom to let Sam stay in our basement until he got himself back on his feet in exchange for him helping around the house, but my mom had repeatedly declined. Although she had known Sam since they were teenagers, they hadn't been close for years, and she thought it would be strange to have him living in our house. But the flood was the last straw. She knew she needed help, and having Sam there was the only solution she could come up with that didn't cost more than she could afford. So the following week, Sam moved into our basement.

Having Sam in our house added a whole new dimension to our family life. His job was to watch us for a few hours on the weekdays after Paula left in exchange for free room and board. He was loads of fun and would often come along when we went on outings with Paula during the day. Sam would give us airplane rides and lift Matthew up onto his shoulders and carry him around the house. He also made a mean chicken parmesan.

With Sam there, my mom had a little more time to breathe, although taking care of my dad was becoming increasingly challenging. His difficulty swallowing had increased to the point where it was hard to get him to eat or drink at all, and he had lost almost forty pounds in the previous three months. His food had to be either mashed up or cut into tiny pieces, and he was often too tired to feed himself. Getting him to the shower was almost impossible for my mom to do alone now, since his walker was no longer sufficient to support his weakened legs, and she could barely manage to get him dressed; although he had lost a great deal of weight, he was still almost 180 pounds. And there was shaving and grooming and exercising his legs to do too.

The neurologist strongly recommended that my mom get a home health aide or nurse to help out a few days a week, but like most people, my dad didn't have long-term care insurance, so my mom realized she would have to pay for any extra help herself. Still, she thought it would be worth it—at least for a little while. That's how Laura came into our lives.

Laura was a tough, wiry home health aide in her late twenties who had a mouth like a truck driver. She came three days a week for two hours at a time, and my dad took to her immediately, as she was extremely warm and compassionate despite her hard exterior. Laura was extraordinarily good at her job, and she had plenty of tricks to get it done in the short time that she had to do it.

On days my dad couldn't walk, she would have him lie down on top of a bath towel on the floor next to his bed, and then drag him all the way down the hallway to the bathroom. Once there, she would hoist him up and onto a shower stool, hand him the soap, and watch him like a hawk to make sure he was washing himself properly. "Don't just sit there," she would holler at him, "or I'm going to come in there and soap you down myself. And you're not going to like it." Amazingly, my dad would follow her orders. We all thought he was too scared of her not to do what she told him.

When it came time for his weekly shave, Laura would climb onto my dad's bed and sit on his legs, holding his head so he couldn't turn it at all. After a minute or two with the razor, his face would be as smooth as a baby's bottom. She would brush his teeth furiously afterward, and was a whiz when it came to changing his sheets, rolling my dad from side to side so she could slide them out from under him and insert clean ones. My mom thought Laura was a godsend, so she gladly overlooked the fact that Laura used the F-word in practically every sentence.

After a few weeks, Matthew and I became quite attached to Laura too. She always had plenty of stories about her various escapades (some of which my mom definitely wouldn't have wanted us to hear), and she always made us laugh. Matthew, who was two-and-a-half at that time and still in diapers, was particularly enchanted by Laura and began to emulate her manner of speaking, including her off-color language. While watching cartoons on the computer, we would hear him suddenly yell, "F***ing Bob the Builder." Other times he would command Paula, "Change my f***ing diaper." It was far from an ideal situation.

My mom was shocked when she heard Matthew speaking like this and would plead with Paula and Sam not to laugh when Matthew used inappropriate language. "It's only encouraging him," she would say, but it seemed they couldn't help themselves. So, of course, Matthew kept it up. Still, our lives had definitely improved with the extra help. And with all of these people in the house, I felt like I was becoming part of a somewhat unconventional but caring extended family.

CHAPTER NINE

The Power of Denial

That spring was also marked by preparations for the Run for ALD. Our dining room table became increasingly covered by paperwork, as well as boxes filled with T-shirts and other items for the September event. My parents and the other members of the board of directors met around our kitchen table every few weeks to ensure that everything was falling into place in the hopes that the run would be a success. So far they were all very pleased by the generosity of those businesses and individuals who had agreed to sponsor the event, and kept their fingers crossed for both good weather and a large turnout. My mom was extremely grateful to the board members for the time and hard work they had been putting in. She realized that she and my dad were very lucky to have this small group of compassionate friends.

Aside from attending these board meetings, my dad still spent most of his time lying in his hospital bed watching cartoons. My mom couldn't tell whether he actually understood what was going on, or whether he just liked watching the colorful animation and listening to the exaggerated voices of the characters. Since he rarely spoke to anyone he saw on a regular basis and usually responded to questions with one-word answers if at all, it was difficult for anyone to tell exactly how much he comprehended about what was going on around him, much less whether he realized how sick he truly was.

One afternoon when my mom and I went upstairs to check on my dad, we noticed that he was watching a show that wasn't a cartoon. He seemed transfixed by what was on the screen, so we began to watch too. We had come in at the end of a movie, we realized, and saw only the final scene—two crying children kneeling before what was obviously their father's gravestone. We both glanced over at my dad, and he had tears running down his face.

I didn't grasp the terrible coincidence or the significance of my dad's emotions then, but my mom did, and her eyes filled with tears. She later told me that she knew then—that at least for that short period of time—my dad understood the gravity of his illness and was aware that he probably didn't have much longer to live. It would have so much easier, she explained, for her to have gone on believing he didn't know.

The fact that my dad was still able to talk on the telephone continued to lead to quite a few misunderstandings, particularly because he was able to speak in such a convincing manner. He would frequently call friends or family members and tell them he was doing things like bowling, shopping, and driving. Those who were not aware of the extent of his disability seemed to believe whatever he told them—even some members of his own family.

One Saturday afternoon when my mom was at work, she received an urgent call from Christine, our weekend sitter, who told her that my dad's sister Patty was on the phone demanding to know why my dad hadn't shown up at the retirement party she had planned for him. My mom was baffled.

"No one ever said anything to me about a retirement party," my mom told Christine.

"Well, Patty said there are a bunch of people at some restaurant in Philadelphia waiting for him to show up for lunch. I didn't know what to tell her. She said that she had made the arrangements with Jack last week and that he knew when he was supposed to be there."

"Well, I guess you're going to have to tell her he can't make it," my mom said with resignation. "Even if I leave work right now, it would take two hours for us to manage to get him dressed and down the stairs, and then drive him all the way to Philadelphia. No one's going to wait that long to eat lunch."

After hanging up the phone, my mom wondered with frustration why Patty had not informed her about the retirement party. After all, it had been less than two months since she had arranged for my dad's therapist to meet with his siblings and impress upon them that my dad was suffering from periods of delusional thinking and was unable to manage his activities of daily living without substantial assistance. They had all sat there in the therapist's office that day—my mom and dad included—while the therapist informed them that in addition to my dad's obvious difficulty walking, he was experiencing significant symptoms of frontotemporal dementia that were not always apparent to people who were not around him for extended periods of time. These symptoms, the therapist had explained, included memory lapses, disorientation, a loss of personal and social awareness (causing the neglect of personal hygiene and grooming, as well withdrawal or apathy in social situations), repetitive behaviors, incontinence, and a general inability to plan or regulate his conduct. My mom had set up this meeting because she had the feeling that Patty and my dad's parents (whom I called Gram and Poppy) still did not understand the full extent of my dad's condition, as they never called her to ask how he was doing or whether he needed anything. She assumed that the reason she never heard from them was either because my dad called them on the phone and told them he was perfectly fine, or that they were still in denial about the extent of my dad's illness.

Either way, my mom fretted, *that meeting was obviously completely worthless. I may just be paranoid, but I feel like they're mad at* me *for some reason, and I don't understand why. Everything was fine before he got sick.*

But early that summer, when my dad was offered the opportunity to stay at his family's summer house at the Jersey shore for a long weekend, my mom was quick to encourage him to go. She packed his suitcase for him and sent him with a detailed note listing all of the activities he would need help with: changing his clothes, showering, shaving, eating, and toileting, to name a few. *When they're around him for a such a long period of time, they'll finally understand the magnitude of his illness*, she thought with relief. *Maybe they'll finally understand what we're dealing with.*

After my dad left for the shore, my mom enjoyed a rare, relatively stress-free few days during which she didn't hear from him. On the afternoon he was supposed to return home, Matthew and I were playing next door at our neighbor's house while my mom stayed home and cleaned. She kept glancing out the window every fifteen minutes or so waiting for my dad to arrive. By dinnertime, when he still hadn't come home, she decided to pick us up from the neighbor's house and headed outside. As she walked out the door, she immediately spotted my dad lying on the driveway with his cane and suitcase sprawled out next to him.

With her heart in her throat, she ran down the driveway to make sure he was alright.

"Jack, are you okay?" she exclaimed, kneeling down next to him.

"I'm fine," my dad answered weakly. "I just can't get up."

As she struggled to help him to his feet, she noticed that he was wearing the same clothes he had been wearing when he had left for the shore several days earlier. It was apparent that he hadn't bathed nor likely used the restroom in quite some time.

"Oh, Jack," she said sadly. "You're a mess. Have you eaten recently?"

My dad shrugged his shoulders.

"Do you know how long you've been lying here?"

"No."

She called out to the neighbor, who had just walked outside with Matthew and me to bring us home. Together, they were able to help my dad up and get him upstairs so my mom could help him change his clothes and bathe.

I literally can't believe this, my mom thought to herself, still astonished at the state in which she had found my dad. *I left a detailed list . . . I guess they didn't look at it. And I don't understand how they could have just dropped him off at the bottom of the driveway without making sure he got in the house.*

Later than night, my mom told my dad, "I guess I shouldn't have let you go. I really thought you'd have fun and everything would be okay. But from now on, you can't go anywhere without me or Laura."

A few weeks later, my dad was placed under hospice care. My dad's neurologist had suggested this option after my dad's health insurance company denied payment for most of his medical expenses on the grounds that he was suffering from an incurable illness that was not covered under the policy. Although hospice came with an uneasy feeling of impending doom, my mom welcomed our new nurse, Cindy, with open arms, as she did the additional benefits of hospice care: a twenty-four-hour hotline to call in case of emergency; a social worker for the family; medication and supplies, including a wheelchair (which my dad now needed to get around most of the time); and a family psychologist to help Matthew and me better understand the concept of death and cope with my dad's illness. Our extended family circle quickly opened even wider to include our new hospice caregivers who would all be coming to our home on a regular basis.

Since my dad had lost more than fifty pounds by this time as a result of his swallowing difficulties, my mom arranged for him to have a gastrostomy PEG tube inserted in his stomach so he could get the food and water he needed for nourishment without having to swallow. My dad welcomed this short surgical procedure, which was performed in early August. By this time, my mom had relocated my dad's hospital bed to our downstairs dining room to make access to him easier for everyone, and his IV pole and feeding bag now stood next to his bed.

The insertion of the PEG tube was a huge relief for my mom, who no longer had to worry about my dad choking or having to cut up his food in tiny pieces. To feed him now, she or one of the nurses or aides would simply elevate the head of his bed, connect the feeding bag to the tube that protruded out of his stomach, and pour a can of protein formula into his IV bag. It wasn't long before my dad began regaining some of the weight he had lost.

At the end of August, my mom surprised Matthew and me by announcing that we—my dad, Paula, and Laura included—were all going to the beach for a long weekend. The plans were to stay in a hotel in Wildwood Crest for two days, and then take my dad to his father's birthday party at Gram and Poppy's shore house. So that weekend we all squeezed into my mom's car, with our luggage and my dad's new wheelchair folded up in the trunk. It was a tight fit, but we made the two-hour drive with no problem.

I was very excited when we arrived at our hotel and saw that we had a two-bedroom suite situated very close to the beach.

"Momma, can Daddy come to the beach with us?" I asked before we had even unpacked.

"Why don't you guys go down to the beach first?" Laura offered. "I'll stay with your dad and feed him, and then I'll get him into his wheelchair and bring him as far down the wooden path to the beach as I can."

"Sounds good," my mom said.

Matthew and I had a lot of fun on the beach, building sand castles and burying each other in the sand. When Laura brought my dad down from the hotel room, she could only get him a few feet onto the beach because the wooden boardwalk ended, and of course she couldn't push his wheelchair in the sand. I sat on his lap in the wheelchair near the edge of the beach for a while, and I think my dad enjoyed being out there in the sun, listening to the ocean. My mom liked being on the beach too and actually relaxed and read a book.

We all went to the beach the next day too, then that night it was time to go to the party at Gram and Poppy's house a few miles away. Paula and Laura came with us, even though they didn't know anyone who would be there.

When we got to the party, there were twenty or thirty people in the back-yard, eating and celebrating. After greeting everyone, we sat down around a large folding table, and Laura pushed my dad over in his wheelchair. We helped ourselves to some platters of food and while we were all eating, and Laura hooked up my dad's feeding bag to his PEG tube and poured his protein drink into the bag on the IV pole. Although my mom had made sure that my dad's family was aware that he could no longer swallow and was getting a feeding tube prior to his surgery, Gram came over and looked at my dad in dismay.

"Where's your dinner? Why aren't you eating anything?"

My dad shrugged but didn't say anything.

"He can't swallow, remember?" my mom told her. "He's actually getting fed through his feeding tube right now." She pointed to the IV pole with the half-full feeding bag.

Gram ignored her and brought over a large plate of shrimp and a fork, and put it in front of my dad.

"Here, eat!" she instructed him.

My dad looked up in surprise. When he didn't begin eating right away, Gram leaned in and stuffed several shrimp into his mouth.

My mom and Laura looked at each other in alarm. My dad started chew-ing the shrimp. When Gram turned away to talk to somebody else, Laura had him spit it out into a napkin.

"I don't get it," Laura whispered. "Why would you put food in the mouth of someone who has a feeding tube?" My mom and Paula rolled their eyes in agreement.

Fortunately, my dad didn't choke during the party, and although he sat quietly in his wheelchair, he smiled and seemed to have a good time with his family. On the car ride home, however, he seemed like he was repeatedly chew-ing on something. When we finally got home, Laura checked inside his mouth and found pieces of shrimp lodged inside his cheeks and under his tongue. "It's a good thing I checked his mouth," she declared. "Who knows what would have happened if he went to sleep with that f***ing shrimp still in his mouth."

My mom shook her head. "Well, all's well that ends well," she said with a sigh. "At least we managed to get away for a few days. Who knows when we'll get a chance like this again?"

CHAPTER TEN

The Run for ALD

With the beginning of September came the highly anticipated Run for ALD. Around a week before the event was set to take place, my mom asked me if I wanted to give a short speech to the people who came to tell them a little bit about my dad and thank them for helping us raise money for ALD research. Never one to be shy, I told her that of course I did! We talked about what I would say while I helped her get everything together that we needed for the big day. There were Run for ALD T-shirts with the names of all of the sponsors on the back, Run for ALD caps, Run for ALD banners, waiver forms for the runners to sign, clipboards, pens, banners, water bottles, bananas, a large tent that we had borrowed, folding tables and chairs, and much more.

On September 8, 2002, we got up at around five in the morning and packed several of the board members' cars and trucks with supplies. Then, after loading my dad's wheelchair into our car, we were off to the Cooper River Park in Pennsauken. We had planned to arrive at least two hours before the 8:00 a.m. registration time to set up, and there was certainly a lot to do. Fortunately, it appeared that the weather was going to be perfect; my mom had nervously checked the forecast every day that week knowing that rain would most likely mean a disappointing turnout, but as dawn broke, it became clear that the day would be bright and sunny.

At the park, I helped set out the bananas and snacks for the runners on a large folding table while everyone else worked on setting up the tent. In addition to the six board members, there were a number of other friends and family members who had volunteered to help out during the event and were responsible for various tasks, like handing out race T-shirts and bottles of water.

A little before eight, just as we had finished setting up, a few runners and some other supporters who came just for the festivities began to arrive. The Run for ALD was finally beginning!

I sat at the registration table with my mom's friends, Carole and Elaine, to greet the participants and check them in. My dad sat to the side in his wheelchair quietly talking with people he hadn't seen in a while as they arrived—old friends and former clients as well as distant relatives. My mom ran around from station to station organizing everything, while Matthew entertained himself by hiding in empty T-shirt boxes under the tent.

The crowd soon grew larger and larger, with runners stretching their legs and jogging around the grassy area to warm up. Others—less serious runners and those who came to watch or support the fundraising efforts—sat in the bleachers near the finish line. Dr. Hugo Moser, the world-renowned ALD researcher and director of the Neurogenetics Research Center of the Kennedy Krieger Institute, arrived from Baltimore to support the event, along with his wife Ann, a highly respected ALD research scientist in her own right.

At 8:30 a.m., the one mile fun walk began. Dozens of people, including a number of children and some older adults, walked together straight down a paved sidewalk for a half mile and then turned around and came back. I walked with my Gramma (my mom's mother) and cousins. Like me, most of the people walking were wearing Run for ALD T-shirts. Some people who were walking with their dogs even dressed the dogs in the shirts!

The race director started the 5k run just after 9:00 a.m. There were over one hundred runners of all different levels. Some were obviously very experienced and sped around the path that circled the park with amazing speed. Others simply walked the entire course, some taking over an hour to finish. Very few people left after they crossed the finish line, most taking seats in the bleachers, enjoying the DJ's music and waiting for the closing speeches and the award ceremony, where prizes would be given to the top three runners in each age group.

Once everyone had finished the 5k, my Uncle David, who was one of the board members, took the microphone and stood before the crowd. After thanking the sponsors and everyone who participated in and came out to support the event, he announced that we had raised over $46,000, the net proceeds of which would be donated to the Kennedy Krieger Institute for ALD research. Everyone sitting in the bleachers broke into applause, and my mom and the other board members were all smiles, as early on the race director had warned them that most first-time 5k runs were lucky to raise even a thousand dollars.

Next, it was my turn to speak. My Uncle David introduced me, and I stood before the crowd.

"Hi, my name is Taylor Kane," I spoke loudly into the microphone. "I just turned four years old in June. My dad, Jack Kane, has a disease called ALD, and he's really sick. There needs to be a cure for ALD. So thank you to everyone who came here today to help us find a cure."

It may not have been a tremendous speech, but as I handed the microphone back to the DJ, I noticed some people in the crowd with tears in their eyes. I felt like they understood how important this day was to my dad.

Dr. Moser spoke next, informing the crowd about the ALD studies that were being performed at the Kennedy Krieger Institute and expressing his gratitude to everyone who had organized and participated in the event.

Finally, the award ceremony began, and prizes were handed out to the three fastest finishers in each age group. And then, just like that, it was over.

There was a palpable sense of joy and accomplishment in the air, as the board members and volunteers helped take down the tent and pack up the supplies. Although it had taken a great deal of hard work and many hours of planning, everyone agreed that the outcome was well worth it. They had managed not only to increase awareness of ALD, but had raised a considerable amount of money to hopefully help find some kind of treatment, or better yet, a cure. A cure that, of course, they all realized would come far too late to help my dad.

A few days later, my mom received a letter from Dr. Moser addressed to all of the Run for ALD board members, sponsors, and participants, which read in part:

> At the beginning of a week that has become renowned for a crime against humanity, my wife and I were privileged to see a group of people unite in an act of total unselfishness and service and pull off a run to benefit the ALD/AMN research and clinical studies that are going on now at Kennedy Krieger Institute.
>
> We wish that there was an answer to this dreaded disease, and we only hope that through your efforts, the day will soon come when no family will have to face the uncertainty with every child's birth that something will be wrong, when we will be able to say "we can make you better," and we will not watch men, strong in their chosen careers, being forced to retire and know that their lives will end prematurely.
>
> We have a long way to go, but each of you has helped bring things a step closer. On the day that the announcement of an effective treatment or cure is made, I hope that we can be present at the first post-cure run and that all of you will stand and take a bow for helping to make the day possible . . .

My mom read the letter aloud to my dad that night as he lay in his hospital bed and told him, "You should be really proud. We all worked hard on this fundraiser, but *you* were the main reason we were able to raise as much money as we did. Almost all of the sponsors and donors and the people who came out to the run were *your* friends, *your* business colleagues, and people whose lives *you* touched. And the fact that you were able to make all those phone calls, hundreds of them, despite how sick you've been, is truly incredible."

My dad smiled broadly, and my mom gave him a kiss on the cheek.

"I really hope that what we've done will make a difference one day in saving the lives of people with this horrible disease," she told him.

CHAPTER ELEVEN

Judgers and Judges

Throughout the fall and winter of 2002, my dad increasingly lost touch with reality. Sometimes he would hoarsely ask why his hospital bed had been moved to one of his friend's houses. Other times he would insist that Laura was his wife and that she was having his baby. Often, when Matthew and I were sitting in his bed to keep him company, he would tell us to hang on tight because he was going to fly us up to heaven. Then, he would hold his hands up as if he were holding a wheel and begin steering.

By this time, we were used to my dad's peculiar statements and behavior and thought it was fun to pretend we were flying in his hospital bed. My mom, on the other hand, was becoming concerned that we would be adversely affected by our continual exposure to what she found to be very unnerving symptoms of my dad's illness. *Am I doing the right thing by continuing to allow the kids to be around him all the time when he's in this condition?* she wondered. *Will they grow up not understanding what's real and what isn't?*

She also felt like she was constantly being judged. Indeed, some people had flat out told her that she should put my dad in a nursing home for our sakes—that it obviously wasn't good for young children to watch their father deteriorate on a daily basis. Conversely, other people were horrified at the thought that she would even consider moving my dad out of the house. What kind of wife would do that? they would ask. Still others expressed dismay that she continued to work instead of staying home to care for my dad full time. My mom didn't know who to believe or what to think.

"I'm damned if I do and damned if I don't," she would tell Paula or Sam or Laura or whoever happened to be in the house at the time she received another unsolicited opinion about what she should be doing differently.

While there were no easy answers, my mom knew in her heart that my dad should be at home, and she truly believed that keeping him there was not only in his best interest, but in mine and Matthew's too. And when she spoke to his doctors, they all agreed that my dad was being well taken care of, and that as long as Matthew and I showed no signs of distress, there was absolutely no reason to separate us from him. We were young and we would be fine, they told my mom.

So we continued on as we had been. My mom was determined to do what she thought was right, no matter what anyone said, and not to let other people's opinions bother her.

Unfortunately, that wasn't always easy. In late October, my mom had been advised by an elder law attorney that she should file a petition to be appointed my dad's legal guardian. She had visited the attorney after my dad had attempted to invest $13,000 in a franchise (which she was fortunately able to quash) and signed us up for a family vacation to Toronto (also intercepted in time). The attorney had advised her that it would be in our family's best interest if she was declared his legal guardian for this and other reasons, including the safeguarding of our family home should my dad ever have to be placed in a long-term care facility.

Filing a petition for guardianship would mean that my dad would have to be declared legally incompetent, the attorney had explained. His immediate family members would have to be notified by mail, and the court would appoint an attorney to represent my dad. That attorney would visit my dad at the house and interview various witnesses in order to determine whether guardianship was appropriate and whether my mom was the proper person to serve as the guardian.

"Okay," she had told the attorney at the conclusion of her consultation, "if you think that's what I should do, then go ahead and prepare the petition."

She had a sneaking suspicion, though, that this decision would not sit well with some members of my dad's family. Plus, she felt like she was somehow betraying my dad by having him declared incompetent. But she also knew that she couldn't disregard the attorney's advice, particularly when doing so could potentially hurt Matthew and me. And she couldn't afford to lose our home.

So that December, my dad's court-appointed lawyer arrived at our house to gather the information necessary for her to determine whether my mom should be appointed my dad's guardian. After interviewing my mom and Paula, the lawyer spoke with my dad, who was in his hospital bed. My dad was in good spirits. When the lawyer introduced herself to him and asked him if he needed anything, he joked, "Yeah, do you have a stack of twenties?" He told the lawyer that my mom was his life and that he knew she was doing everything she could for him. After he had answered a few questions, though, he stopped responding to the lawyer, and began to stare blankly into space like he often did with us. The lawyer eventually gathered her things and told my mom she was planning to interview some of my dad's family members over the next month or two, and then she would be submitting her recommendation to the judge. So now there was nothing to do but wait.

The holiday season came and went without incident, but also without my dad dressing up as Santa for my cousins and Matthew and me, as he had always loved to do. We went to see Gram and Poppy and all of my dad's siblings in Philadelphia on both Christmas Eve and Christmas day, despite the fact that it was being becoming more and more difficult for my mom to get my dad down the front steps of our house and into the car. Even though my mom had always been quite physically strong, without help from another person with equal (or preferably greater) strength, like Sam, my dad would somehow end up on the ground next to the car door, and at that point it was almost impossible to lift him back up and into the car. Fortunately, that Christmas Eve and Christmas she had plenty of help, and we were able to attend mass at my dad's childhood church, something he clearly enjoyed. No one spoke of the guardianship petition, and we all enjoyed the holidays.

At the end of January, we celebrated Matthew's third birthday around my dad's hospital bed with just our immediate family, Laura, and our hospice nurse, Cindy. My mom had bought Matthew a vanilla sheet cake, which she placed on a table right next to my dad's bed so he could see it. But when she turned to get matches to light the candles, my dad reached his arm out and put his hand right through the cake! Even though the cake was destroyed, Matthew didn't seem to mind. We figured my dad must really have wanted some cake, so we put some icing on his lips so he could have a taste. He actually seemed to be able to swallow a little better, and Cindy promised me that I could help her try feeding him some soft, easy-to-chew foods the following week.

A few days later, my mom took Matthew to a dental appointment to have several cavities filled in his baby teeth. She had been referred to a special pediatric dentist in a nearby town for this procedure since it had been determined that Matthew would have to be placed under sedation. On this, their third visit to this particular pediatric dentist, after sitting in the waiting area for at least an hour, my mom and Matthew were finally called into the room where the procedure was to take place.

The dental assistant helped Matthew into a large reclining chair and told him she would be strapping a "piggy nose" around his head and over his nose, and that he was to breathe through the piggy nose. (The piggy nose was actually a bubblegum-scented mask shaped to look like the nose of a pig through which nitrous oxide, or laughing gas, was administered.)

Matthew was clearly scared to death. He began screaming and fought to get out of the chair. As my mom tried to calm him down, the dental assistant called in two additional assistants and instructed them to hold Matthew down while she strapped on the mask. Matthew still wasn't having it. Crying hysterically, he flailed his arms and legs, and whipped his head from side to side so strenuously that the dental assistant wasn't able to strap on the mask. The dentist, an elderly, stoic-faced man, appeared at the doorway as the three women fought with all of their might to hold Matthew down. The dentist sternly told Matthew that he'd better behave himself. As the dentist approached the chair to try to strap on the mask himself, Matthew started shrieking at the top of his lungs, "No f***ing piggy nose! No f***ing piggy nose ever!"

The dentist's eyes appeared to bulge out of his head as he stared at Matthew in horror. He yanked my mom's hand and dragged her down the hallway and into the room of another patient around Matthew's age, who was calmly sitting in a dental chair and obviously enthralled at the prospect of getting his piggy nose strapped on.

"This is how normal children act," the dentist hissed at my mom, pointing to the other young boy. "I am not going to fill your son's cavities today with his appalling behavior."

Mortified by Matthew's use of the F-word (she thought she had gotten this problem under control), my mom sheepishly tried to explain. "He's just really scared. There's been an ongoing situation at home and . . . "

"Obviously," the dentist said. "I've noticed that your husband hasn't come to any of Matthew's appointments. When a father is too busy to make time for his child's medical needs, the child is going to act out. You really should speak to your husband and reschedule this appointment for a day when he can come with you."

At first, my mom was at a loss for words. Then, when she managed to process what he had said, she became angry. "I won't be rescheduling the appointment," she told him. "And how dare you criticize my husband for not being here. For your information, he has a terminal illness and he's confined to a hospital bed. You really shouldn't be jumping to conclusions about people you don't even know."

With that, she hurried back to the room where Matthew was still crying in the dental chair, picked him up, and carried him out of the office to her car.

My mom was still upset the next day when she described what had happened to Paula. "The dentist obviously thought I was a horrible mother. I guess I can understand that with Matthew acting the way he did, but I can't control what people say around him when I'm not home all day. And for him to say what he did about Jack . . . it was just so rude. And since when do both parents take their kids to dentist appointments anyway?"

"They usually don't," Paula assured her. "Regardless, I wouldn't lose any sleep over the situation. Why don't you just look for a different dentist?"

"Matthew's too scared right now, and quite frankly, I don't really think it's necessary. He just has little cavities in a few baby teeth that will probably fall out soon anyway. I don't think anything terrible is going to happen if he doesn't get them filled."

Fortunately, my mom was right. Matthew's baby teeth fell out soon after, and his permanent teeth came in perfectly fine. (He also never got another cavity again.)

In February, the judge granted my mom's application to be appointed my dad's legal guardian. Although my mom was relieved that the entire proceeding was over, she was somewhat dismayed when she learned that of the witnesses interviewed, one—my dad's sister—had opposed her appointment as guardian. While it obviously didn't affect the court's ruling, my mom was still extremely dismayed by this obvious slight.

"If she doesn't think I should be the one to take care of him," my mom said on more than one occasion, "I'd be happy to send him over to her house, hospital bed, feeding tubes, catheter, and all. She's more than welcome to take over as his guardian."

Of course we all knew my mom was kidding. Well, sort of. Because over the last year and a half, she'd come to realize that caring for someone who is seriously, chronically, terminally ill on a daily basis is often a thankless job—

both physically draining and emotionally exhausting in a way that only those who have been there can truly understand.

CHAPTER TWELVE

In the Eye of the Storm

With February 2003 came one of the largest snowstorms to ever hit South Jersey. As the first snowflakes started to fall, my dad experienced his most frightening medical crisis to date. Sam was the first to notice something was wrong and yelled for my mom to come to his bedside. My dad appeared to be in a great deal of pain, and his face was drained of color.

"Jack, are you okay? What hurts?" my mom asked him with urgency.

My dad didn't respond. His breathing appeared to be very irregular.

"What do you think is going on?" she asked Sam.

"I have no idea."

My mom felt my dad's forehead. No fever.

"I think we have a digital blood pressure monitor somewhere upstairs," my mom said. "Maybe we should take his blood pressure."

She found the monitor, and Sam wrapped the cuff around his arm.

"One sixty over one ten. I think that's pretty high, isn't it?" he asked.

"I think so. Isn't it supposed to be one twenty over eighty? Let me look it up on the internet."

After a few minutes of searching, my mom exclaimed, "Oh no, according to these articles on the internet, he's practically in a hypertensive crisis! What do you think that means?"

"I don't know," Sam responded. "Maybe he's having a stroke or a heart attack. I don't know, but something's definitely wrong. I know we can't call an ambulance since he's on hospice, but is there anyone we can call? It's Sunday and the roads are already covered with snow. Who's going to come out now?"

"You know Lori? Her father is Jack's neuropsychiatrist, and he lives right down the street. He's been very accommodating to us. I'll call him and see if he can come over."

The doctor agreed to come right over. In the meantime, Sam took my dad's blood pressure again.

"It's worse. One seventy over one twenty."

"Oh my God. I'm scared. What if he's dying right now? He's still not responding at all."

They waited nervously for ten minutes or so, checking my dad's blood pressure every few minutes.

When the doctor finally arrived, brushing the snow off his coat and shoes, he quickly strode to my dad's beside and performed a thorough examination. It wasn't long before he turned to my mom and Sam with a look of resignation on his face.

"I'm not sure exactly what's going on, but he's definitely in a semi-comatose state. There's a good chance he only has a few days left to live. You should probably notify his family or anyone else who would want to come and say goodbye."

My mom was shocked. While my dad had been on hospice for almost eight months, he had seemed to be doing relatively well. She certainly didn't expect something out of the blue like this to happen. She said a silent prayer. Then, after thanking the doctor for coming out in the snow, she put in a call to the hospice hotline and was told a nurse would be sent out the following day, if at all possible, given the forecast for close to two feet of accumulating snow. She also called my dad's family to inform them of the doctor's dismal prognosis.

"What do we do now?" she asked Sam.

"We'll just take turns sitting up with him until tomorrow, I guess. Then we'll go from there."

"But what if . . . it happens tonight? The governor has already declared a state of emergency from today through Tuesday, and the roads are going to be completely impassable for the next day or so. No one will be able to get to our house, not even an undertaker, and we won't be able to leave either. What if he dies and we're all stuck in the house with him? I don't want Taylor and Matthew to be trapped inside the house while he's lying dead in another room!"

"Don't panic. I doubt that's going to happen," Sam said, attempting to reassure her. But, of course, neither of them knew what was going to happen.

At around midnight, my mom tried to get a few hours of sleep while Sam sat by my dad's bedside, talking to him and watching television. My dad's blood pressure had stabilized by then, and although he was still nonresponsive, he seemed to be resting more comfortably.

My mom took over at around 3:00 a.m. "He doesn't seem to be any worse," Sam told her. "Maybe he had a stroke or something and now it's over."

"I guess. He's still doesn't even seem to hear us, and he's not moving." She was exceedingly thankful to have Sam there now, as she couldn't imagine going through this alone. "Thanks for staying up so late," she told him. "You should get some sleep."

My mom sat beside my dad's hospital bed for a while, then stood up and walked to the front door to look outside. Everything was covered in a thick blanket of snow. The road wasn't visible at all, and she estimated that the snow must have accumulated at least eighteen inches, as it looked to be halfway up her car door. She tried to push the front door open to get a better view, but the door wouldn't budge. *We're really snowed in*, she nervously thought. *There is definitely no way anyone will be able to reach us if Jack takes a turn for the worse.*

I feel like we're sitting ducks. I don't care if it's still snowing, I'm going to start shoveling the driveway now.

So, she got on her winter coat and gloves, opened the garage door, and began shoveling, determined to get a path cleared on the driveway before sunrise. The snow was extremely heavy, and although it was quite cold out, my mom became heated and exchanged her coat for a hooded sweatshirt. Every twenty minutes or so, she went back into the house to check on my dad. His condition remained unchanged. So she kept shoveling.

While my mom never liked snow, or the cold weather for that matter, she enjoyed being outside in the black of night, shoveling. It was peaceful, and the strenuous physical activity kept her from worrying as much about my dad as she would have if she were sitting by his bed, obsessing over every twitch and groan. She continued shoveling for over three hours, finally clearing one side of the driveway completely, just as the sun began to rise.

As she surveyed her work, moving her hair off of her face with a wet glove, she noticed a snow plow slowly coming down the street, billows of snow shooting off to the sides of the road in its wake. She smiled with relief; at least my dad had made it through the night, and hopefully soon the roads would be drivable. Maybe the hospice nurse would even make it over later to try to figure out what was wrong with him. My mom went inside and stripped off her ice-laden sweatshirt, boots, and gloves, put on a pair of sweatpants, and climbed into the hospital bed next to my dad.

When she woke up several hours later, my dad was awake and staring at her.

"Hi," he said faintly.

"Hi. Are you feeling better?"

My dad struggled to clear his throat and nodded.

My mom got out of bed and wrapped the blood pressure monitor around his arm.

"One thirty over eighty-five. I think your blood pressure is almost back to normal. That's good." She got up and crushed his daily medication with a mortar and pestle, mixed it into his protein drink, and filled his feeding bag with the mixture.

"Here's your breakfast," she said as the concoction traveled through his feeding tube. "Just rest. I'm going to go get a shower. I'll be back soon."

By the time my mom came back downstairs, Sam was up and standing by my dad's bed.

"He seems a lot better," she told Sam. "He's not saying much, but I think whatever happened yesterday seems to have passed. His blood pressure is back to normal."

"He must have either had a heart attack or a stroke."

"Yeah, it was definitely something pretty serious. But hopefully he'll prove the doctor wrong, at least for a while."

As it turned out, my dad beat the odds and survived this crisis. Although no one was able to determine with certainty what had happened to him that February day, he slowly regained his strength, and after a few days was right back to where he was before it had happened. My mom felt extremely fortunate—not only because my dad had survived, but because she and Sam had managed to deal with the situation without Matthew and me ever realizing how close we came to losing him that day.

CHAPTER THIRTEEN

Life in a Bubble

During much of my dad's illness, my mom felt that she was living in a bubble. Inside the bubble was her life at home, with the round-the-clock caregiving, the unrelenting stress, and the various people who were in and out of our house helping care for my dad. Outside the bubble—beyond the invisible layer separating her from the outside world—was everything and everyone else. Normalcy. Life. The way things used to be. Even though she traveled outside the bubble almost every day when she went to work and occasionally to run errands, it felt strange. Strange to be doing normal things like driving and working and eating lunch and shopping when all the time she was worrying about what was going on inside the bubble.

The people outside the bubble looked at her differently now. They also treated her differently. A coworker, for example, would be talking about what a horrific weekend she had had because one of her newly manicured fingernails had broken while she was gardening, and then she forgot to pick up garlic at the grocery store and had to go back in the midst of cooking dinner to get it— and then look at my mom and suddenly stop talking, obviously realizing that her own problems seemed trivial when compared to my mom's. My mom was embarrassed that people felt they had to watch what they said around her. "It's fine," she would assure them. But at the same time she would think to herself, *I can't believe someone would actually get that upset over a broken fingernail or*

about forgetting an item at the store. How can people worry about such insignifi-
cant things? I guess when I think about it, I used to let those types of things bother
me before too, but I feel like a completely different person now—like I have nothing
in common with regular people.

When friends or coworkers would ask how my dad was doing or how she was managing at home, she couldn't tell them the truth. As much as she didn't like being secretive, how would people react if she said, "I spent most of last night with this guy who lives in my basement trying to attach Jack to a Hoyer lift so we could change his sheets"? Or, "I was late to work because Jack pulled the feeding tube out of his stomach, leaving a big hole which caused the entire contents of his stomach to pour out all over his clothes and sheets, making a huge mess that took two hours to clean up"? Or, "The sitter accidentally left the phone on Jack's bed and he ordered a subscription to *Playboy* for the home health aide whom he thinks is pregnant with his baby"? Telling the truth was simply out of the question. So when she spoke to people who were outside the bubble, she simply told them, "Jack's holding his own. And we're doing fine, thanks for asking." But of course we really weren't.

My mom was eternally grateful for those people who were inside the bubble with her. They saw it all; they knew how we lived. She could tell them anything. They helped when she needed help. They worried with her when things weren't going well. They laughed and made life more fun. They cared for Matthew and me like we were their own. They made everything bearable. And it wasn't only Paula and Sam and Laura and the hospice nurses. There were others. Many of whom were unexpected surprises—people my mom and dad rarely saw or hardly knew before my dad got sick.

One of those people was our next door neighbor, Gran. Her real name was Ann, but she told Matthew and me to call her Gran because she had grand-children our age. The nickname stuck, and everyone in our house called her Gran too, even my mom. Gran had lived next door to us for years—ever since my parents moved into the neighborhood—but she and my mom had hardly ever spoken, mostly due to their diverse schedules and different stages of life.

But now that Gran's mother was on hospice, she and my mom had something in common. They compared caretaking techniques, borrowed one another's medical supplies, and talked about their futures. Gran also became friendly with Paula and Sam, and was a frequent visitor at our house. My mom went to her house too, sometimes late at night when Matthew and I were asleep, and she and Gran would talk into the wee hours while polishing off a bottle of wine. Gran became like a real grandmother to me while my dad was sick, and I always had fun playing with her granddaughters when they came to visit.

There was also my Uncle David. He was my dad's third cousin, a bit younger than my mom, and while he was always present at family functions, they didn't socialize much before. But after my dad was diagnosed with ALD, Uncle David always showed up when my mom needed assistance. He helped her take my dad to doctors' appointments, drove all the way over from his house in Philadelphia to help her pick my dad up when on several occasions he fell and there was no one else around to help, and called regularly to check in and see how my dad was doing. On Mother's Day, he even brought my mom a gift—a T-shirt adorned with a picture of Matthew and me—because he knew that otherwise she would have received nothing at all and the day would have gone by unacknowledged. My mom always said that that shirt was one of the most thoughtful gifts she had ever received, and that Uncle David was one of the most considerate people she had ever known. At the time, I wasn't so sure. After all, whenever he came over, he would repeatedly chant, "Taylor Kane is a pain." But I eventually realized he was just trying to be funny, and I came to appreciate his big heart. Uncle David was also a huge part of the Run for ALD and worked extremely hard to help raise money for ALD research along with the rest of us.

Another frequent visitor was one of my dad's childhood friends, Dennis. He came over every week or so and sat with my dad, even after my dad could barely speak and was quick to lose focus, often turning his head away to stare blankly at the cartoons on his television when others were talking to him. Sometimes, Dennis would bring Ronnie, another mutual childhood friend. The two of them would entertain my dad with stories about their past escapades while growing up in South Philly, and there was always laughter coming from the dining room when they came. These visits were one of the highlights of my dad's existence.

My mom was particularly grateful for the companionship Dennis and Ronnie provided my dad because it was rare for any of his other close friends to visit. Although my mom understood that my dad was not the best company given his condition and that people were busy with their own lives, she was disappointed that more of his friends didn't reach out—at least once in a while—even to come by for a few minutes. My dad would repeatedly ask her about certain friends with whom he had been particularly close, wondering how they were and what they were doing. She would tell him she didn't know. But what she did know was that at least some of them weren't really too busy.

One friend with whom my dad had been particularly close for many years lived in our neighborhood. My mom and I would see him taking his daily walk right across the street from our house almost every evening. Yet he never stopped by, never even looked in the direction of our front door. After my dad had asked about him several times, my mom sent his friend a letter, telling him my dad wasn't doing well and really wanted to see him. There was no response. Several times when I saw my dad's friend walking, I called out his name, but he didn't even look over. When my mom eventually confronted him and told him how much his absence was hurting my dad, he told her that he simply couldn't bear to see my dad in his current condition. My mom was a bit annoyed by this response and told him so.

"Jack asks for you over and over," she said. "Maybe you should think about his feelings right now instead of your own. I don't like seeing him this way either, but I do. Every day. You were such close friends, and you know he would have been there for you if the roles were reversed."

My mom's plea didn't work. We didn't see my dad's friend again. My mom thought he had probably started taking his daily walks in the opposite direction.

"Your dad was the kind of person who was always thinking about other people," she later told me. "He would never hesitate to visit friends who were sick and try to cheer them up and make them laugh, no matter how sick they were. But some people just can't face illness. They don't know what to say to someone who's sick, or maybe it reminds them that they could get sick too."

Fortunately, we had some very special people who were able to overcome whatever fears or discomfort they may have had, and who were there for us through thick and thin. They came into our bubble to support and comfort my dad—by talking to him, making him laugh, or just holding his hand without saying a word. But like many people faced with a medical crisis come to learn, our support system was comprised of very different people than those my mom would have expected before my dad got sick. "It's just like the old saying," she would tell me, "you never know who your true friends are until there's a crisis."

CHAPTER FOURTEEN

My Fifth Summer

Shortly after the Run for ALD the previous September, my parents and the rest of the board of directors decided they would make the fundraiser an annual event. By the summer of 2003, several new members had joined the board: Sam, my mom's friend Lori, and Lori's husband, Paul.

As in the previous year, the board meetings for the Second Annual Run for ALD were held around our dining room table. Before each meeting, several of the board members would help my dad out of his hospital bed and into his wheelchair so he could sit at the table too, for at least a portion of the meetings. Although my dad was not able to participate in the planning this time, he took great pleasure in sitting there quietly among this large group of friends and just listening. At every meeting my mom allowed him to have one beer—which she poured into the IV bag attached to his feeding tube. Since the beer bypassed his mouth and trickled through the tube directly into his stomach, she thought it was unlikely that he could taste it. But my dad claimed he could and seemed to relish the fact that he could once again enjoy a beer with his friends. Although my mom wasn't sure the hospice nurses would have approved, no harm ever came of it.

The planning for the Second Annual Run for ALD came much easier than the year before, since this time everyone knew what to expect. But there was still a lot to do, and they didn't have my dad to help. My mom was in charge of sending out all of the fundraising letters to the previous year's sponsors and invitations to the participants, and I helped her seal the envelopes and put stamps on them.

By this time, I knew that my dad was probably going to die soon. Since the beginning of the year, a hospice bereavement counselor had come to our house to meet with me and try to help me prepare for my dad's death. Together we read stories about the circle of life in animals and humans, and talked about grief and loss. The counselor told me that when my dad died, he would not physically be with me anymore, but that he would live forever in my heart. I tried to comprehend that.

My mom tried her best to prepare me too, and explained that my dad would be leaving us and going to heaven—which I knew was the place where he had always tried to fly Matthew and me in his hospital bed. I didn't really know when this would happen or what to expect, but I knew when he went there, I wouldn't have a dad anymore.

I also didn't know that my mom was secretly worried that my dad might not live to see the second Run for ALD in September. He had been suffering from repeated urinary tract infections, which the hospice nurses thought may have been caused by the fact that he was constantly pulling the tubes of his catheter out. So far, the antibiotics had kept these infections in check despite the raging fevers that accompanied them, but there was always a danger that one day he might not be so lucky. The doctors had instructed my mom to increase the dosage of one of my dad's medications to try to decrease his compulsion to pull out his tubes, but his obsessive behavior was becoming more and more difficult to manage.

My dad also began putting various items in his mouth—strings he pulled off his blankets, the tags on his pillow, stuffed animals, and the like—and attempting to chew or swallow them. My mom was afraid he was going to choke, and we had to be extremely careful not to leave anything near him, like the crayons Matthew and I used while coloring in my dad's bed. She found some large plastic toys for him to chew on, and for a time, whenever we went in to see my dad, he had a huge plastic cookie sticking out of his mouth.

My mom received conflicting advice as to whether she should use wrist restraints to secure my dad's wrists to the rails of his hospital bed to prevent him from pulling out his tubes or choking on pieces of his blankets. She tried the restraints for a short time, but we all felt so bad seeing my dad struggle to move his hands that she quickly decided that the restraints would have to go, and that everyone would just have to repeatedly check on him throughout the day and night. After that, my dad's care truly became an around-the-clock effort, and either she or Sam would stay up most of the night, sitting by my dad's bedside.

Bedsores were also a major concern since my dad was now completely unable to reposition himself. Not only could bedsores cause painful skin ulcers, but they could potentially lead to a deadly infection. Once my dad began getting these pressure marks on his heels and his back, he had to be rolled from one side to the other every two hours. My mom began coming home from work during her lunch hour to check on my dad and help Paula reposition him, or change his sheets, empty his catheter bag, or do whatever needed to be done.

By this point, my dad had stopped speaking entirely. When he tried to communicate with us, it was by using his fingers. We would tell him to hold up one finger for "yes," and two fingers for "no." This seemed to work well, although sometimes he got a bit confused when Matthew or I would pepper him with questions. Still, it was better than nothing, and it seemed as though he could still understand what we were saying to him.

Despite everything that was going on with my dad, the atmosphere in our household remained surprisingly upbeat. My mom insisted that we all make the best of the situation and live as normally as possible, and for the most part we did.

I was particularly sad, though, when I graduated from daycare that June and my dad couldn't come to my graduation ceremony. My daycare friends and I had practiced for several weeks for the big day, and when it arrived, we excitedly stood in front of our parents and relatives, wearing our caps and gowns. And while my dad wasn't there, Paula, Sam, and my mom were in the audience to support me. Still, I couldn't wait to get home and tell my dad all about it and show him my diploma. "In September," I told him proudly that evening, "I'm going to be starting kindergarten."

My dad gave me the thumbs up sign.

Two days later, I celebrated my fifth birthday! My mom had planned a small party and rented a giant inflatable water slide, which she had set up in our backyard. She invited some close friends and relatives, Paula and her twin boys, Sam and his two children, and Gran and her grandkids. Before the party started, we hung a sheet at the entrance to the dining room so none of the kids would feel scared or awkward if they saw my dad lying in his hospital bed.

The weather was cool for the end of June, and it was a bit rainy, but that didn't stop everyone from having a great time. We all put on our bathing suits and slid down the giant slide into the pool of water at the bottom over and over again—even my mom and Sam tried it! In between our turns on the slide, we ate pizza and played games. Then, my mom lit the candles on my cake and everyone sang "Happy Birthday" to me.

My birthday party was truly the highlight of that summer, although Matthew and I also had a lot of fun whenever my mom or Paula or Sam would take us next door to go swimming in Gran's pool. And even though I was looking forward to kindergarten, I didn't want the summer to end.

CHAPTER FIFTEEN

The Beginning of the End

July and August went by much too quickly. My dad was still holding his own, but my mom was concerned about how she was going to get him to the Run for ALD, which was scheduled for September 7. Since she and the other board members had to get to the park several hours before the event started in order to set everything up, she was worried that my dad would not be able to make it through the long morning. Fortunately, Sam was able to arrange for an ambulance service to bring my dad to the event shortly before the start time and to stay at the park in case of emergency.

Like the first Run for ALD, the second one went off without a hitch. Again, the weather cooperated, and hundreds of friends and acquaintances showed up to participate or offer their support. My dad was able to sit in his wheelchair throughout the entire event, although this time he didn't seem to recognize many of the people who came to talk to him and just nodded his head to acknowledge their presence. I spoke to the crowd again at the end of the 5k run, and Uncle David announced that we had raised $30,000 for ALD research.

A few days later, I started kindergarten! I was attending a school within walking distance of our house and was so excited to meet my new teacher and make new friends. My mom walked to school with me the first day and stood outside with the other mothers, and a few fathers, who were huddled around the front door, waiting for our teacher to take us in the building. When it was time to go, she gave me a big hug and told me she would be back to pick me up when the day was over.

My mom later told me she stood there for a little while with several of the other mothers, quietly shedding tears as she watched me walk into the school with my new class. Unlike the others, though, her tears were brought on not only by the conflicting emotions of watching her firstborn child go off to school, but by the fact that my dad couldn't be there to witness this huge milestone in my life.

As I had expected, I loved kindergarten. I quickly made new friends, and my teacher, Mrs. Gibson, was so nice to me. Her husband had recently passed away, and since she somehow knew about my dad's illness, she always made sure to check in with me to make sure I was okay. September and October passed by quickly.

On Halloween, I dressed up as an angel and marched in my school's parade with all of my new classmates. Later that day, I went out trick-or-treating with Matthew, who was dressed in a devil costume. Sam, who thought my dad should be able to join in the Halloween fun, dressed him up like a sailor, drawing a fake mustache on his face and a tattoo on his arm with washable marker.

"I don't know how I feel about that," my mom said when she saw my dad lying in his hospital bed adorned in his Halloween makeup. "I suppose he would probably get a kick out of it, but somehow it just seems wrong." My dad had a huge grin on his face, though, so she let him the keep the tattoo. But she wiped off the mustache.

That Halloween was one of the very last times my dad smiled. Within days, his feeding tube began to back up, and his heart rate and breathing began to slow dramatically. Sometimes more than a minute would go by between his breaths. Cindy and the other hospice caregivers said that my dad's internal organs were likely shutting down. An oxygen tank was brought in, and he was hooked up to a number of monitors. He began moaning frequently and seemed unable to recognize anyone around him, instead staring straight up at the ceiling. Matthew and I were scared.

Cindy told my mom that she didn't think that my dad would live for more than a few more days, given that he was displaying many of the clinical signals of impending death. Although my dad had been on hospice for almost sixteen months, the fact that the end was so near for him still came as a shock to everyone. My mom tried to steel herself for the inevitable. She went into work that day and told her boss the situation and that she would need some time off. When she got home, she took me into my bedroom and closed the door. "Taylor," she said quietly, "Daddy is probably going to die very soon. If you want to spend some time with him and tell him how much you love him, you should do it now. If you're afraid, though, you don't have to. He already knows."

I wasn't afraid. I just wanted to be with my dad.

When I went in to see him that afternoon, I climbed up on his hospital bed and kissed his cheek. "Goodbye, Daddy," I whispered with tears running down my cheeks. I wrapped my arms around him and lay there with him until I fell asleep.

Over the next few days, Laura, who had been so devoted to caring for my dad, also lay beside him in his bed, sometimes for hours at a stretch—far past the time she was scheduled to stop working. Sometimes Paula, my mom, and I would all climb in the bed with them. Sam would stay up with my dad at night, holding my dad's hand and talking to him. My mom called the priest at my dad's church, who came to our house to perform the last rites. Cindy and our team of hospice caregivers came to our home more often, instructing my mom and Sam how to administer morphine, since my dad appeared to be in some discomfort.

By the end of the week, though, my dad's condition hadn't changed. His feeding tube was still backing up, he was still moaning (the hospice nurses told us this didn't mean he was in pain, but it was very disturbing nonetheless), and he was noticeably losing weight, causing his already pale face to appear drawn. His brothers came to say goodbye to him, as did his friend Dennis.

Two more weeks went by, and still no change. My dad's persistent moaning was so loud it kept us up at night. My mom and Sam were still administering morphine as well as my dad's other medications every few hours and checking his respiration and pulse regularly.

When my dad's neuropsychiatrist visited one day, he wrote a prescription for sleeping pills and implored my mom to take them so she could get some sleep. My mom was afraid to try them in case she was needed in the middle of the night.

The priest came back and performed last rites a second time.

Our household was fraught with tension. I began to feel like I couldn't swallow.

Cindy urged my mom to stop giving my dad all liquid nutrition and fluids. "You're only prolonging the inevitable," she told my mom.

My mom didn't know what to do. She, Sam, and Paula talked about this dilemma incessantly when the hospice caretakers weren't there.

"I feel like if I stop giving him fluids," my mom told them, "I'll be the one responsible for killing him. When we went to his priest last year, Jack told him that he wanted to be kept alive no matter what. How can I in good conscience go against what he wanted?"

"Maybe we should just give him less than usual, like half the amount we normally do?" Sam suggested.

"I just don't know. Jack's doctors told me that when he said he wanted to be kept alive by any means possible, he was probably suffering from dementia. But I still think he really meant it."

"Well, what if the fluids are just making him more uncomfortable?"

My mom ultimately decided that they would stop giving my dad the protein supplements but continue to give him fluids, hoping that this option might somehow keep him alive while allowing his internal organs to heal. She knew that this choice may have not been medically sound, but she felt stuck in a quandary, trying to balance two equally objectionable alternatives.

They all agreed that that seemed like a good compromise.

The next time Cindy came to our house, she brought my bereavement counselor with her to try to help me try to deal with the anxiety I had been experiencing. I explained to the counselor that I felt like I couldn't swallow and that my stomach was queasy a lot of the time.

"We have a hospice facility not far from here," she told my mom after talking to me. "Maybe you should consider moving Jack there. This is an incredibly difficult situation for all of you to be in right now."

"But I really wanted him to be at home with us until the end," my mom said. "I don't want him to be in a facility where he doesn't know anyone."

"Our hospice facility is really fantastic. He would be very well cared for."

"Well, how much longer do you think he can continue to live in this condition? You guys told me almost a month ago that you were pretty sure he only had a matter of days left to live."

"Maybe he still has some unfinished business here that's stopping him from letting go," Cindy interjected. "Perhaps there's someone he wants to see one last time?"

My mom thought about it, running through a list of names in her mind. "I don't know, maybe his mother? Or another extended family member—but I'm not sure who that could be."

"It is unusual for someone in his condition to hang on this long," Cindy admitted. "If you decide you want to transfer him to our inpatient hospice facility, just let us know. It may be for the best—you've all been through an awful lot."

Another week went by. My dad had lost more weight and looked extremely haggard, but otherwise there was still no change. My mom had been operating on only a few hours of sleep for the past five weeks and said she was semi-delirious. "I'm going into work for a few hours," she told us one day. "I'm pretty sure they assumed I was only going to be out a week or so, not over a month, and my desk probably has two-foot-high piles of paperwork sitting on it. I'm going to bring some work home—I feel like I'm being so irresponsible by missing this much time."

I was having problems in school now too. My anxiety had gotten worse, and I felt like I was having problems breathing and swallowing every day. Mrs. Gibson understood what I was going through and would comfort me and bring me water whenever this happened, but I didn't know what was causing it or how to make it stop. When I finally told my mom what was going on, she make a quick decision to have my dad moved to the hospice facility, at least for a little while.

"I think it's time," she told me. "We'll still go see Daddy every day after school."

She informed Cindy of her decision. "I don't think we can take anymore," my mom said sadly. "I didn't want to have to do this, but living with so much constant stress is obviously affecting the kids now. It's just gone on too long. Christmas is only a little over a week away, and I want Taylor and Matthew to be able to be happy that day without having to hear their father moaning or worrying about him dying. Maybe we can bring him back home after Christmas if he's still . . ."

"You're making the right decision," Cindy told her. "I promise, a nurse will be checking on him around the clock."

"Can you make sure they don't withhold fluids? I really don't want that."

"Of course. They'll follow whatever instructions you give them."

The next day, my dad was taken out of the house on a stretcher. My heart sank. I began to cry. My mom and Sam both looked like they were going to cry too.

CHAPTER SIXTEEN

My Dad Gets His Wings

That night, my mom and Sam followed the ambulance that carried my dad to the hospice facility to check him in and make sure he would get proper care. The next morning, we all went back to visit him. It was sad seeing my dad lying there in a barren room, decorated only by the family pictures my mom had placed next to his bed. He looked so ashen and frail, somehow even more so than he had in our dining room. Although his eyes were open, it was clear that he didn't realize we were there. We stayed for a little while, talking to him and holding his hand, then went back home. We knew his siblings were planning to visit that day, and we were comforted by the fact that he wouldn't be alone. My mom went back again by herself later that night.

Adjusting to being in our house without my dad wasn't easy. It seemed so quiet. By force of habit, time and time again I would run into the dining room to see him, only to be startled by the sight of an empty hospital bed, a feeling quickly followed by the sinking realization that he was truly gone.

We visited my dad at the hospice facility the next two days. Then on that third night—December 20, 2003—my mom and I were sitting on the couch watching television together, when Cindy, who had a key to our house, suddenly appeared in our family room.

"I'm so sorry," she said somberly. "Jack died a little over an hour ago."

I don't recall much of what happened next, but I remember screaming and crying and throwing up at the same time. My mom put her arms around me to stop me from shaking while Cindy cleaned up the mess.

"I wish I would have known . . . I wanted to be there at the end. I feel so bad that he was alone," my mom said.

"You were there almost nonstop for weeks. You did everything you could for him. And he went very peacefully," Cindy told her, giving us both a big hug.

After she left, my mom told me she was going to go down to the basement to break the news to Sam and that they would both talk to Matthew together. I went upstairs to my room and laid on my bed surrounded by my stuffed animals. I knew that things would never be the same again.

We celebrated Christmas five days later at my Gramma's house. All of my cousins were there, and I was able to forget about my dad and enjoy myself for a little while. But not for very long—my dad's funeral took place just two days later.

Despite our young ages, my mom never seriously considered the possibility that Matthew and I would not attend the funeral. After everything we had seen and lived through during my dad's illness, she felt that we were as prepared as we could be, and that it was important for us to get a sense of closure. My bereavement counselor and I had discussed what happens at funerals and burials on a number of occasions, so I knew what to expect, and I wouldn't have missed my dad's funeral for anything. When it came to Matthew, who was still only three, my mom's main concern was whether he would be able to sit still and stay quiet for such a protracted period of time. The bereavement counselor had thought Matthew was too young to benefit from counseling, and my mom knew that he still couldn't grasp the concept of death, so she didn't think the funeral would overly upset him. But to make sure he was occupied, as she was choosing a casket for my dad and planning his service over Christmas week, she made sure to pick up some extra sticker books and crayons for Matthew to take with us to the church.

On the morning of the funeral, a big black limousine pulled up at our house. Paula, Laura, and Sam all piled in with my mom, Matthew, and me. Riding in a limousine somehow made our journey seem even more important and overwhelming than it already was.

When we arrived at my dad's childhood church in Philadelphia, we were ushered into a downstairs basement so that Matthew and I didn't have to stand in the long receiving line before the funeral. Paula and Sam stayed with us while my mom went upstairs to stand by my dad's casket for the viewing. I was surprised when I noticed my hospice bereavement counselor walking down the basement steps—I didn't know she was going to come, but I was so glad that she did. She assured Paula and Sam that if Matthew needed to come back downstairs during the service, she would be happy to stay with him.

As the two-hour viewing ended, we all went up to the church to sit in the first pew with my mom and await the beginning of the funeral. My mom wanted Paula, Sam, and Laura to sit with us since they had been like family throughout my dad's illness, and also to keep an eye on Matthew in case he got fidgety during the service.

The church was filled to capacity. So many of my dad's friends and relatives were there, as were his former coworkers and clients, several of his doctors and nurses, and even his friend who would walk past our house without looking over. "Now he shows up," my mom said under her breath, shaking her head. But, still, it was heartwarming to see how many people's lives my dad had touched.

The funeral service passed by in a blur, but I clearly remember when it came to a close and we stood up to follow my dad's casket as the pallbearers pushed it down the long church aisle. My mom carried Matthew in one arm and held my hand with her free hand, and as we slowly walked behind the casket, I looked around at the faces of the people still sitting in the pews. Many were looking back at me with tears in their eyes, some openly weeping. I was suddenly struck by the strange beauty of this tragic situation—the fact that all of these people who had been a part of my dad's life understood, cared, and shared in my grief, comforted me and brought me a sense of peace.

At the cemetery later that afternoon, I stood with my mom and Matthew and watched as my dad's casket was lowered into the ground. I slowly walked over and put a single flower on the casket. "Goodbye forever, Daddy," I whispered.

My parents on their wedding day in 1997. They were married
at my mom's church in Cherry Hill, New Jersey.

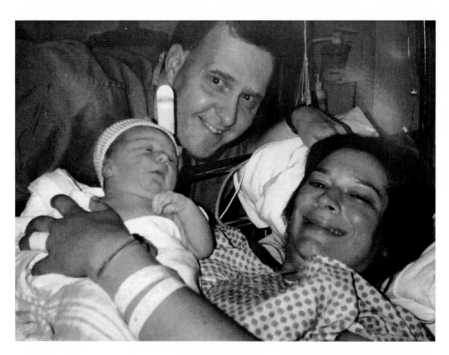

I was born on June 23, 1998. I was named after my mom's favorite author, Taylor Caldwell.

Before my dad got sick, we were inseparable. I cried a lot as a
baby, but my dad always knew how to calm me down.

This is my favorite picture of my dad and me. He always used
to play with me on the swingset in our backyard.

Here I am with my dad's identical twin brother, my Uncle Jimmy (left) and my dad
(right). When I was young I had trouble telling the difference between them.

This is a picture of my dad, my brother Matthew, my half-sister Tina, and me, shortly after Matthew was born. Tina and I often wonder whether our dad would have been strict or laid-back during our rebellious teenage years, and if he would have intimidated our boyfriends.

At Gran's pool. My terrible twos. I'm still wondering why nobody fixed my sunglasses.

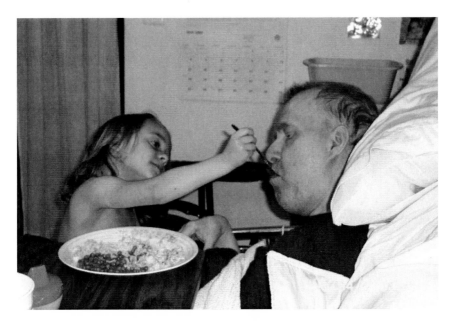

Before my dad completely lost his ability to swallow, I would
help the hospice nurses feed him mashed-up food.

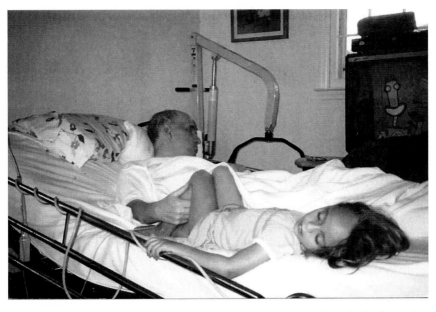

When my dad was still able to still talk, he would tell my brother and me that his hospital
bed could fly, and that if we sat on his bed he would fly us to Heaven. Looking back, I know
he didn't realize what he was saying, but at the time Matthew and I loved flying with him.

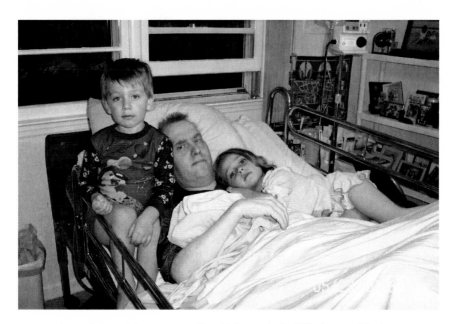

As my dad got sicker, my mom found it increasingly difficult to get Matthew
and me to leave his side. Children are often shielded from loved ones who are
dying, but I'm so glad my mom let us spend so much time with him.

My dad was buried in Belmawr, New Jersey. It became a tradition for us to visit
my dad on Father's Day, his birthday (September 12), and at Christmas-time.

And my mom memorialized every visit!

We continued the Run for ALD even after my dad passed away. Here I am at the fourth annual event, speaking to the crowd to raise awareness of ALD.

Here I am again, at the Run for ALD several years later, singing a song dedicated to my dad.

Signing up new members for Hero Club, which I founded my freshman year of high school.

This was the second time I visited GW as a prospective student. I was so happy to be on campus again. At this point, I was absolutely sure I wanted to attend.

My mom and Keith got married in August 2015. I was so glad Keith was officially joining our family. I surprised everyone with a rap song I wrote about my mom and Keith's relationship.

This picture was taken during Lobby Day at "Rare Disease Week on Capitol Hill 2016," hosted by the EveryLife Foundation for Rare Diseases--one of the first ever rare disease events I attended. I visited my New Jersey legislators' offices and asked them to support legislation that improves the lives of rare disease patients and their families.

My high school graduation in 2016. I graduated in the top 10% of my class! My art teacher helped me create my graduation cap for me. (Notice the "Hi Dad" at the top).

This was taken on the "blue" carpet at the Global Genes Tribute to
Champions of Hope Gala in 2017. I felt like a movie star!

Here I am in 2018 posing with a zebra at a rare disease event in D.C.. The zebra
is the nationally recognized symbol of rare disease, due to its unique stripes.

PART TWO

In addition to ALD, there are a number of other rare, X-linked recessive diseases, including Hemophilia A and B, Duchenne muscular dystrophy, Becker muscular dystrophy, Kennedy disease (SBMA), Alport syndrome, chronic granulomatous disease (CGD), and Hunter syndrome (MPS II), just to name a few, which were long considered "male-only diseases." For years, females were thought to be simply genetic carriers who silently passed the defective gene on to their male children, and who themselves were completely asymptomatic. Unfortunately, for many of these diseases, this long-standing belief has proven to be untrue. In addition to the fact that carriers of X-linked recessive diseases have a 50 percent chance of passing the defective gene on to each of their offspring, it has only relatively recently been recognized that many females do, in fact, develop physical symptoms of the disorder, sometimes severe and disabling ones. Because there is so little medical research when it comes to females who carry the gene for these diseases, however, and because they are rarely included in clinical trials, doctors often attribute women's symptoms to other disorders or misdiagnose them as being psychological in nature. X-linked carriers may thus be subjected to years of physical problems without ever knowing their true origin, whether there are any preventative measures they can take to stave off the onset of symptoms, or if there is any effective treatment.

When it comes to ALD, recent studies have shown that females who carry the defective gene have as much as an 85 percent chance of developing physical symptoms of the disease, typically beginning after age thirty-five. Although these symptoms are usually less severe than those experienced by males and only rarely include cognitive impairment, they can nonetheless be life-altering and debilitating. Symptoms differ from female to female and may include weakness, stiffness and spasticity of the legs, joint pain, and bowel and bladder dysfunction. Women who experience these symptoms often struggle to find doctors who are familiar with ALD, much less ones who recognize that their symptoms are related to the disease.

Female carriers of many of the other X-linked recessive diseases face similar diagnostic challenges. While the nature of the symptoms and their prevalence vary from disease to disease, one thing is clear: There is an urgent need for more research that focuses on females with these genetic disorders. These women—who already face difficult reproductive decisions, particularly when the procedures to avoid passing on the defective gene can cost thousands of dollars and are often not covered by health insurance—must no longer be dismissed as "just carriers."

CHAPTER SEVENTEEN

Coping and Moving On

After my dad died, my house—like my heart—felt incredibly empty. My mom replaced my dad's hospital bed with our old dining room table, which had been in storage for the past eighteen months. Serving dishes and china once again lined the shelves where his medical supplies had been stacked. Still, the dining room held so many memories of my dad it was hard for me to go in there at all. I also missed the daily hustle and bustle of the home health aides, nurses, and counselors, especially Laura and Cindy. It seemed so quiet without them. My mom told me that Sam would probably be moving out soon as well. I felt like I was losing much more than my dad.

"Everything will be okay," my mom assured me. "It will just take a little getting used to."

But I wasn't so sure. I went back to kindergarten after the winter break ended, and Mrs. Gibson, who had heard what had happened, tried to console me. "Your dad and my husband are together in Heaven now," she told me. "They've probably become close friends and are having a great time trading jokes and playing cards together." That thought did make me smile. I could always count on Mrs. Gibson's comforting hug to get me through the school day. Although I still had some difficulty swallowing and breathing as a result of my continued anxiety, as the months went on and I focused more on kindergarten and my new friends, my symptoms eased. I began to feel more normal.

One day that April, as I was walking home from school with Paula and Matthew trailing a half block behind me (I insisted on being independent and walking by myself), I noticed something unusual in the overcast sky above my head. It appeared to be a giant eagle—not an actual bird, but dozens of bright stars that formed the shape of an eagle—slowly moving closer and closer, then hovering above me. I had never seen anything like it before, but its presence was unmistakable, and in that instant I somehow knew that my dad was with me. I didn't understand exactly what I was seeing, but I wasn't afraid. I felt a sense of warmth rush over me. *Daddy*, I thought, *you really are here.* I had never been as sure of anything in my life as I was that the eagle was my dad. I stood perfectly still and, with a lump in my throat, watched as the eagle began soaring away, rising higher and higher into the clouds, until I could no longer see it.

"Taylor!" I heard Paula exclaim as she and Matthew strolled up beside me. "Why did you stop walking? What's wrong?"

"Nothing," was all I was able to say. I'm not sure why, but I didn't want to tell her or Matthew what had just happened, at least not then. I walked the rest of the way home with them, reflecting on what I had experienced. I felt like something had changed inside me—almost like a weight had been lifted off of my heart.

After we got back to the house, I thought about the eagle for the rest of the afternoon as I waited patiently for my mom to get home from work. As soon as she walked in the door, I followed her into the kitchen. "Momma," I said in a half whisper. "I saw Daddy when I was walking home from school."

"What do you mean?" she asked me.

"I saw a giant eagle flying right above my head. It was Daddy."

My mom looked at me curiously. "Why would you think an eagle was Daddy?"

"Well, it wasn't a regular eagle. It was made of stars. A lot of really bright ones. And I don't know how I knew it was Daddy, I just did."

My mom didn't laugh or dismiss what I had seen as a figment of my imagination. "Well," she said, "I guess it probably was Daddy trying to show you that he's okay up in Heaven, and that even though he's not physically here, he will always be with you."

"Have you seen him, Momma?"

"No. But sometime kids can see things that adults can't."

"Do you think I'll see him again?"

"You might. I don't really know."

I never did see the eagle again, although I thought about it many times after that day. I still think about it sometimes. Although the notion that the eagle was actually my dad might seem far-fetched to some people, to this day I have never questioned what I saw or what it meant. After all, when it happened I was only five years old and wasn't searching for signs from Heaven or some type of physical evidence that my dad somehow lived on. I was hardly able to comprehend death at that point, and was simply too young to even have conceptualized the prospect of an afterlife.

While I can't say that the experience made my grief instantly disappear, the eagle became a source of great comfort to me. From that time on, I knew without a shadow of a doubt that my dad was watching over me and that his spirit would be with me forever. That knowledge opened my heart and mind, and gave me hope. And although I never had another "visit" from my dad again, over the years I have often sensed his presence. Sometimes it comes when I'm having a bad day and suddenly notice what feels like a reassuring hand resting on my shoulder. Other times, when I'm sad or depressed, the song "Sweet Home Alabama" unexpectedly starts playing on the radio, bringing an instant smile to my face. And frequently, I just have an inexplicable feeling that my dad is still with me, giving me strength and encouragement.

Losing someone you love is incredibly difficult, and moving forward can be even harder. But I learned an important and life-changing lesson on that spring day fifteen years ago: Our loved ones never truly leave us.

CHAPTER EIGHTEEN

Children Grieve Too

Just after I began second grade, my mom told me we would be moving after the end of the school year. I was devastated, to say the least.

"Why do we have to move?" I repeatedly asked her. "I love my school and my friends here. I don't want to leave them."

"I just think it would be for the best," my mom said. "I never really liked this neighborhood. And besides, it would be good for us to get a new start, in a different house."

"But what if no one likes me there and I don't make any friends?"

"Taylor, don't be ridiculous. You always make friends easily wherever you go. And we'll be in a neighborhood with more kids your age for you to play with. Here, most of our neighbors' kids are already grown."

The knowledge that we were going to move put a damper on my second grade year. My mom spent a lot of time fixing up our house and deciding what to do with my dad's clothes and personal belongings, saving some things for Matthew and me and donating others to Goodwill. The upcoming move also meant that we would be leaving Gran behind, and Paula as well, since we would no longer need her full time once Matthew was in first grade.

On the last day of the school year, I woke up feeling despondent. This would likely be the last time I would ever see the many friends and teachers I had come to adore. It would also be the last time I would ever see Mason, the boy who I'd had a crush on for the entirety of that year.

I had never spoken to Mason, but I watched him play soccer during recess, and I knew he was the best soccer player in the school. I told myself that I would go up to him during recess that day and tell him how I felt. I rehearsed what I was going to say in my head. *"Hi Mason. You don't know me, but my name is Taylor. I have a crush on you, but I am moving to another town next week. I just wanted to tell you that. Bye."*

Perfect, I thought.

As I sat through my last second grade lunch period, I felt increasingly nervous. I ate my ham and cheese sandwich and imagined all the things that could go wrong. After I said my piece, Mason might look at me in shock and turn away. He might laugh at me, maybe make fun of me in front of the whole school. By the time recess arrived, my misgivings had gotten the best of me, and I decided not to say anything. I spent my last recess collecting acorns with my friends.

As if squandering my last chance to talk to Mason wasn't bad enough, moving day arrived just two days later. As my mom was driving Matthew and me to our new house (which was actually only a few towns away), I tearfully exacted a promise from her that gave me a little bit of solace.

"If I don't make any friends after a month, will you let me go back to our old neighborhood and move in with Gramma and PopPop? I could still go to my old school then and see my old friends."

"Oh, Taylor," my mom exclaimed in an exasperated tone of voice. "Fine," she said after taking a few deep breaths. "I promise. But *you* have to promise to give our new neighborhood a chance. I really think you'll like it if you just keep an open mind."

As usual, my mom turned out to be right. I loved our new house, even though my bedroom and closet were both much smaller than they had been in the old house. On the plus side, we had a playroom and a bigger backyard with a built-in pool. As my mom had assured me, there were plenty of kids in my new neighborhood, and both Matthew and I quickly made friends, many of whom would come over to swim and play.

I easily settled into my new grade school as well. Matthew and I had to take a bus because we weren't within walking distance of our school anymore, and my mom hired a new sitter to stay with us after school until she got home from work.

Although I was happy in my new life, I still missed my dad and thought about him every day despite the fact that almost two years had passed since his death. For a long time, I didn't tell any of my new friends or teachers what had happened to him. I wanted so much to fit in, and not having a dad made me different from everyone else. I was also determined to keep his death a secret so I wouldn't have to face all of the inevitable "I'm sorries" and pitying looks I knew I would get if people found out. But one day in June, my teacher announced that we would all be making Father's Day cards for our fathers. My heart dropped. As my classmates began making their cards, I tiptoed over to my teacher's desk and quietly told her that my dad had died and I had no one to make a card for.

"Oh, Taylor, I'm so sorry," she said.

"Thank you," I replied.

"Do you have a grandfather you can make a Father's Day card for?"

"Yes, I do." I returned to my desk and began coloring a card for my PopPop. A few minutes later, Charity, the girl sitting at the desk next to me, raised her hand.

"I've never met my dad," she told the teacher. "He's been in prison ever since I was born. Can I make a card for my uncle?"

"Of course you can," the teacher replied.

On the bus ride home from school that day, I sat next to Charity and told her, "I don't have a dad either. My dad died."

She smiled at me, and we instantly became best friends.

This pattern repeated itself several times during my early years. On the rare occasion I met someone my age who had lost a parent, we inevitably developed an immediate bond, instinctively understanding how the other felt. We both knew we had something in common—something profound and indescribable that none of our friends could truly comprehend—and would unwittingly gravitate toward one another.

I later learned from my mom that Matthew also experienced a similar sense of isolation from his peers, as well as anxiety that they would learn what had happened to our dad. She told me that one day, when Matthew was in third or fourth grade, he brought home a blank family tree to complete for a homework assignment. When she sat down with him to help him fill in the blanks, Matthew asked her if he could invent a "fake father who was still alive" to write in so he didn't have to include my dad's name and the year he died on his family tree.

"Why would you want to do that?" she asked him incredulously.

"I just do," he said.

My mom admitted that at first she was taken aback because she couldn't understand why Matthew would be ashamed or embarrassed that his father had died. But after a while she realized that Matthew just didn't want to be viewed as "that kid in the class without a father" or singled out by having to answer uncomfortable albeit well-intentioned questions about what had happened. She eventually convinced him to include our dad's name on his family tree, but to omit a date of death so as not to draw attention to the fact that he was no longer living.

In addition to the isolation I felt, in the early years after my dad's death I also went through a phase where I suffered from uncontrollable fear and panic attacks. It was difficult for me to put into words at the time, but I remember it as an overpowering terror that something horrible was about to happen—to me, my mom, Matthew, or one of my friends. Because I didn't experience this fear until the third or fourth grade, I didn't immediately relate it to my dad's death. I'm not sure what brought it on, but one day I suddenly became convinced that something bad was going to happen to my mom. I was nervous—to the point of panic—whenever my mom wasn't home, imagining that she was going to get into a car accident or have a heart attack, or fall victim to some other catastrophe.

I remember one evening in particular when I called my mom on her cell phone every five minutes while she was at a work function, begging her to come home because I was certain she was going to be shot by a random intruder. My mom repeatedly told me she was fine and would come home as soon as she could, but her reassurances didn't alleviate my anxiety. I spent the next few hours sobbing and throwing up, with our poor babysitter holding back my hair while she tried to calm me down.

There were similar episodes, a number of which involved panic attacks, hysterical crying, and uncontrollable vomiting. Being told that it was statistically unlikely that something bad would happen to my mom did nothing to alleviate my anxiety. After all, my dad's diagnosis and death from ALD was even more improbable. It took me quite a while to work through my perpetual worry that tragedy was lurking around every corner.

Matthew experienced similar fears. While he had seemed relatively unaffected by my dad's death at first, when he got a little older, he would tearfully climb into bed with my mom at night, telling her that he was afraid that he was going to die when he went to sleep "just like Daddy did." Of course, my mom would try to reassure him that this wasn't going to happen, but her words didn't convince him. For a while, she didn't have the heart to force Matthew to go back to his own bed because she knew he needed comfort, so she let him sleep next to her every night. But after some time had passed without any indication that Matthew intended to return to his own bedroom, she broke down and bought him a puppy that he was allowed to sleep with, as long as he stayed in his own bed. Surprisingly, it worked.

Losing my dad triggered other emotions too, like anger (Matthew) and guilt (me), which appeared during different stages of our development. But mostly there was a sense of sadness—at first all the time, then, as the years went on, more often on holidays and at milestone events like birthdays and graduations.

From what I've read and learned through experience—both personally and years later as a counselor at a bereavement camp—many of the feelings Matthew and I had over the years were typical childhood reactions to grief. Indeed, it is not unusual for children to experience intense fear and separation anxiety at some point following a loss. And that's understandable: With the death of a loved one, children lose their innocence and are forced to face the grim reality that the world is a dangerous place where bad things can happen at any time to themselves or those close to them. Feelings of alienation, loneliness, and self-consciousness are common in children as well. Unlike most adults, children often have an overpowering desire to fit in with their peers and don't want to be viewed as being different in any way. As a result, their loss becomes a painful secret that must be internalized so as not to evoke any unwanted attention or scrutiny.

Grief is a complicated mixture of emotions, especially in children. Unfortunately, it is often overlooked or misinterpreted because it is different than adults' grief and it is expressed in different ways. It may not appear to be as intense right away because it doesn't come on all at once—often, children relive the loss time and time again as they grow older and begin to more fully appreciate its impact on their lives. And it's not one size fits all; every child experiences grief in his or her own way. It may take many years, and sometimes requires the help of a professional, for children to work through their feelings and to come to terms with the loss.

Over the years, I've had people ask me what they should say to a child who has lost a parent or other close family member, or what they can do to help. I think that people are often too afraid of saying the wrong thing or unnecessarily reminding the child of the loss by bringing up the name of the person who died. Personally, I always loved when people who knew my dad shared an anecdote about him or told me something about him I otherwise wouldn't have known. The fact that people remembered him fondly always made me feel better; I never grew tired of hearing stories about my dad and seeing him through the eyes of others. I also appreciated it when people told me that I reminded them of my dad. "You have his smile," I heard frequently, or "you must have inherited your dad's outgoing personality." These observations always made me feel like my dad was still a part of me—that he was somehow living on through me. My favorite compliment of all: "Your dad would be proud of you." That one may have meant the most because it was something I knew I would never actually get to experience for the rest of my life.

When it came to people who didn't know my dad, or people I was meeting for the first time, I always appreciated a simple "I'm sorry," although I have to admit that these two words were said so frequently I became a little numb to them. But still, it was always nice to know someone cared.

As for what not to say . . . For me, it was not particularly helpful to hear "your dad is in a better place" (*how is it better when he's not here with me?*), "at least you got the chance to say goodbye to him" (*yes, when I was five*), or "don't be sad—you'll be with him again one day" (*like that thought should seriously make me feel better right now?*). The worst, though, was when people told me that I was lucky that I was so young when my father died. They would usually pronounce that at age five, I could not have truly appreciated or understood what I had lost, or that my bond with my father would have been stronger, and my loss therefore greater, had I been older. "Imagine how much more difficult it would have been if you were a teenager when your dad died," I heard on a number of occasions.

While I understand why people might believe that tragedy is easier to bear at a young age, I do not believe that this is necessarily true. For me, and I suspect many other children who have lost a loved one, the deepest pain comes not as much from the too-short relationship that was lost, but from the relationship we will never have the opportunity to experience—the endless thoughts of *What would it have been like?* and *I wish he/she would have been here too . . .*

The one thing I know for sure: There is no good or easy age to lose someone you love.

CHAPTER NINETEEN

Finding My Voice

For the next several years, I felt like death followed me wherever I went. By the time I was in fourth grade, ALD had taken my Uncle Jimmy's life, and Gram and Poppy had also passed away. My mom tried to persuade me not to attend the funerals because she thought it would upset me too much, but I insisted on going. I loved my uncle and grandparents and wanted to be there to honor their memories. I also remembered how much it had comforted me to see how many people attended my dad's funeral, and I felt that it was important for me to be there.

By this time, I had reconciled myself to the inevitability of death and the need to somehow finding meaning in loss. At each of these funerals—as I said goodbye to Uncle Jimmy first, then Gram a year later, then Poppy several months after that—I tried to remind myself that all three were free of pain now and reunited with my dad. I also did my best to remember the lessons I had learned from my bereavement counselor and to focus on the manner in which they had lived, rather than how they had died. Although the funeral services were incredibly sad, I also found them moving because I was able to gain a much deeper understanding of the lives these members of my family had led, the things they had accomplished, and they people they had touched. I learned things I never knew before, such as the fact that Gram was a much-loved high school gym teacher for many years, that Poppy was a well-regarded labor leader, and that Uncle Jimmy had worked extremely hard throughout his life to become the CFO of an international corporation.

Learning more about Gram, Poppy, and Uncle Jimmy made me realize that I really didn't know that much about my dad's life. Of course, my mom had told me the basics: I knew that he grew up in a row home in Philadelphia and became a lawyer in his mid-twenties. I also knew that he was a kind and outgoing person, a caring father, and that he had a great sense of humor. But now, I wanted to learn more. Over the next few months, I repeatedly engaged my mom in conversation about my dad.

"Momma, what was Daddy's favorite color?

"Blue."

"What was his favorite season?"

"He liked fall and winter the best. He didn't like hot weather."

"How about his favorite food?"

"Pizza. Or maybe chicken and mashed potatoes."

"Did he like living in New Jersey?"

"Not really. He always loved living in Philadelphia. He liked the liveliness of the city—being able to walk everywhere and sit out on his porch and watch the people passing by."

"Why did he live in New Jersey then?"

"Probably for me. He knew I was a Jersey girl, and I didn't want to live in the city."

"Was he happy when I was born?"

"Of course he was. He was thrilled. He used to rock you in my rocking chair when you were a baby, and he always told me how beautiful he thought you were. He adored you."

Hearing that made me smile.

"Taylor," my mom said, "your dad was honestly the best person I ever met. I never heard him say a negative word about anyone. Ever. He loved to help people. When he was walking around Philly at night, he would pick up complete strangers who were passed out on the street and help them get home or somewhere safe. Clients would call him at two o'clock in the morning with some kind of personal problem, and he always took their calls. He had so many friends, from prominent politicians and businessmen to blue-collar workers and people who were homeless and didn't have a dime to their names. Everyone was equal in his eyes. Your dad was truly one of a kind."

"Why did he have to get ALD?" I asked. "It's so unfair."

"He was born with it," my mom said, "just like Uncle Jimmy. And no, it isn't fair, but actually Daddy and Uncle Jimmy were both pretty lucky because a lot of boys who are born with ALD die when they are around your age. At least Daddy and Uncle Jimmy got to grow up and experience life, get married, and have children."

I nodded to let my mom know I understood.

"Anyway," she continued, "after Daddy was diagnosed, one of his main goals in life was to find a way to help the doctors and scientists who are studying ALD find a cure. He knew that wouldn't happen in time to save him, but he wanted to do whatever he could to try to make sure that no more young boys would lose their lives. That's why we started the Run for ALD."

"How does the Run for ALD help?"

"Two main ways. First, we try to raise awareness of the disease. Most people have never heard of ALD because it's so rare. Many doctors haven't even heard of it. So when a boy begins to develop symptoms, like vision or hearing problems, or starts to have difficulty in school, ALD is usually not even considered. The doctors may think that the boy simply needs glasses or has attention deficit disorder or something like that. Then, after his condition keeps getting worse and a specialist finally discovers that he has ALD, it's too late for him to get a bone marrow transplant, which is the only thing that can stop the disease from progressing. A bone marrow transplant is a treatment where a sick person's bone marrow is replaced with bone marrow taken from a healthy person. But it doesn't work unless ALD is diagnosed very early on, before significant symptoms develop."

"So, if more people knew about ALD, like parents and teachers and doctors, they might be able to figure out right away that a boy had it, and he could be cured?"

"Yes, that's the idea. The transplant itself is very risky, but right now it's pretty much the only chance to stop the disease. The other thing Run for ALD does is raise money for research. Doctors and scientists are trying to find better ways to stop ALD—something that is safer than a bone marrow transplant and will help boys who already have serious symptoms, as well as grown men like Daddy. Bone marrow transplants are much more dangerous in adults with ALD and usually don't work very well. But it takes money for that research to happen, and it's hard to raise money for rare diseases like ALD, because people usually donate money to help fund research for diseases that affect someone they know or someone in their family."

I thought about what my mom had told me. Even though for the past several years I had been very reluctant to talk about what had happened to my dad, I felt determined to somehow help further this cause that had been so important to him.

"I want to raise awareness of ALD too," I told my mom. "I can tell people about it, like my friends and my teachers."

"I think that would be a great idea. Daddy would have loved it. Maybe you could hand out some flyers about the Run for ALD in school and see if any of your teachers or classmates would be interested in coming this year."

"Okay. When can I start?" I asked excitedly.

"Well, the run this year is being held on April 29, which is only a few weeks away, so if you're going to do it, you have to do it soon. But we're going to have to get permission from your principal first. Do you want me to talk to him, or do you want to?"

"I'll talk to him myself."

Later that week I summoned up the courage to go to my principal's office, tell him about my dad, and ask permission to hand out flyers promoting the upcoming Run for ALD. The principal readily agreed. In fact, over the next several days, he personally accompanied me to every classroom in the entire school to talk about ALD and to invite all of the students to attend the run. It was actually fun going from room to room and telling the students and teachers about ALD, and the fact that I got to miss math and science made it even better.

When April 29 finally arrived, I was overjoyed to see that a group of my classmates and teachers had come to participate in the Run for ALD, and to learn that many parents of my classmates had donated money to help support ALD research. I also felt incredibly empowered by the knowledge that my efforts had actually made a difference, and that the money I helped raise would go toward finding a cure for this horrific disease.

A month later, my principal asked me to speak about ALD at my elementary school graduation ceremony. With all of my classmates and teachers present, and an audience of hundreds of parents and grandparents, I stood at the microphone told my story: how a rare disease called adrenoleukodystrophy had taken my dad's life, and how important it was that people come together to support research efforts for rare diseases like ALD. I ended my presentation by singing a Luther Vandross song called "Dance with My Father," which is about a child who lost her father and longed desperately to dance with him just one more time. And while I may not have been the best singer or hit every note perfectly, I saw many teachers and parents with tears running down their cheeks as I sang. When I finished, I was rewarded with a standing ovation from the entire auditorium. People had actually listened!

I didn't realize it at the time, but the end of my fourth grade year marked the beginning of a new chapter in my life. From that time forward, I made it my mission to carry on my dad's legacy by helping to spread awareness of ALD and doing whatever I could to raise money for ALD research. Instead of keeping my story a secret, I realized that by talking about it, I could help other people while making my dad proud. Working to achieve those goals gave me a sense of purpose. It became my new passion. It helped me to heal.

CHAPTER TWENTY

Taking the Bad with the Good

I entered middle school that fall with a renewed feeling of self-confidence. Even though I was now in a much larger school with students I'd never met, I no longer had the sense that I was an outsider around my peers, nor did I feel the need to keep my past a secret. Sharing my story had given me both a sense of newfound freedom and an awareness that I could actually help other people. Classmates I barely knew began to come to me for advice when a parent or other relative became ill or passed away, knowing that I could empathize with their feelings. I quickly learned that like my dad, I had a knack for comforting others by offering them my understanding and support.

Helping other people helped me too. Not only did it feel good to brighten someone else's day, I also felt that I was honoring my dad's memory by trying to live my life in the way he lived his. I knew I wanted to do more, and I repeatedly begged my mom to help me find other ways I could make a difference in our community. My mom thought about it for a while and agreed to take me to some local nursing homes to see if they would let me visit some of the residents in need of company.

It didn't take long for us to find an assisted living facility that not only welcomed me, but put me on a weekly visitation schedule. I was a little nervous at first, so my mom came with me while I visited some of the residents in their rooms. I needn't have worried. Everyone I visited was so happy to have me there, many telling me about their own lives and families while I sat next to their beds and listened. Some wanted me to read to them, and others just to talk.

After my first few weeks, I got up the courage to do "my rounds" on my own, so my mom dropped me off at the front door of the nursing home and picked me up a few hours later. I had some amazing conversations and learned a great deal about the past from some of the elderly residents, although I often felt a little sad when some of them told me how much they wished their own children or grandchildren would visit. That always reminded me of how my dad longed for his friends to visit him more often when he was sick. And although I couldn't replace their family members, I knew the residents looked forward to my weekly visits.

Toward the middle of fifth grade, as my mom began preparations for the Fifth Annual Run for ALD, which was scheduled for May 10, I decided I wanted to put my dad's battle with the disease on paper and describe how it had affected my family. At the time, I often wrote fictional short stories for fun ("My Bus Driver Is a Robot" is one that I still remember), and my mom told me I was a good writer, so I set out to write something more meaningful that would educate others about ALD.

I found an old notebook in my mom's office, tore out the used pages, and got to work. Writing my story took months. I relived as much as I could remember of the previous eight years in vivid detail as I wrote, and although the process was often difficult, putting my memories to paper was also cathartic. Periodically, I asked my mom for comments and suggestions. I also asked my English and homeroom teachers at school for their input and to help with editing. In the end, I decided to call my story "'Dancing with My Father': My Story About Life, Loss, and ALD." The story was simple: It covered my life before, during, and after my dad's battle with ALD, as well as how important I felt it was for people to attend the Run for ALD and raise money for research to help find a cure.

After it was finally finished, I gave the completed version to my mom and asked her to check for grammatical errors (as an English major, my mom insisted on making sure Matthew and I knew how to write properly, frequently complaining that our schools did not focus enough on grammar as the schools did in her day). I watched her read my story as I nervously waited for her verdict.

"Taylor, this is really good!"

"Thanks, Mom. I think my teachers liked it too."

"I think we should send it to a local magazine. Maybe an editor will read it and be inspired to advertise the Run for ALD in the magazine. If the date and location of this year's run were mentioned, a lot more people would know about it and hopefully participate. And we could raise more money for research."

"Do you think my story's good enough?"

"I do. And it can't hurt to try."

My mom found a well-regarded local magazine that most of our town's residents received in the mail on a monthly basis, and I wrote a letter to the editor, enclosing a copy of my story and asking if she would consider sharing information about the Run for ALD in an upcoming issue.

When we mailed the letter, neither my mom nor I expected to hear back anytime soon, if at all. So I couldn't have been more surprised when the magazine's editor called our house a few days later and asked to speak to me. I listened in amazement as she told me that she wanted to publish my entire story—word for word—in the March issue of the magazine. After providing some details about photos and deadlines, she asked to speak to my mom. As I handed over the phone, I could barely contain my excitement over the fact that my hard work had paid off to a greater extent than I had ever expected. Now my whole town would know about my dad and ALD!

When the March issue of the magazine was published a few weeks later, I felt very proud. My story looked so professional, and there were pictures of my dad and me in several places throughout the article. The location and date of the Run for ALD were featured prominently beneath my story, and my mom told me she thought it would surely attract more people to come to the event.

Over the next month, we heard from several families from New Jersey and neighboring states who had read my story and wanted us to know that they had sons or brothers or other relatives with ALD and would be attending the run in May. Because ALD is so rare, we had never actually met anyone outside our own extended family who was affected by ALD, and neither had the families who contacted us. (This was before Facebook and other forms of social media became popular modes of seeking out and connecting with other people.) Although it was sad to hear their stories, my mom and I were glad that we would have the opportunity to bring these ALD families together. I could hardly believe that my story had served as the catalyst.

On the downside, the publication of my story also caused me a great deal of personal heartache. Several girls in my grade saw the article and taunted me mercilessly one day on the bus ride to school. They told me that my lips and cheeks were so red in the half-page headshot of me that accompanied my story that it looked like I was wearing makeup (I wasn't). The girls shrieked with laughter discussing my picture, calling it "ugly" and "hideous," and informing me that they would be writing their own stories for magazines that would be far better than mine.

To say I was upset by these comments would be an understatement. No one had ever said such mean-spirited things to me before. I was on the verge of tears for the entire day. When I got home and looked at the magazine picture in the privacy of my bedroom, I saw the same thing that the girls had seen— my lips and cheeks did appear overly red. I realized that everyone who saw the story probably thought I was wearing makeup. I was mortified.

I took the picture to my mom, crying.

"I hate this picture so much," I sobbed. "I look so ugly."

"The picture's nice," she said. "Why do you hate it all of the sudden?"

"Some girls were making fun of me on the bus. They saw the picture and said I looked like I was wearing makeup. And they're right."

"Come on, Taylor, you are beautiful. I don't think it looks like you're wearing makeup—it's just a colorful picture. The girls are obviously just jealous or insecure about themselves. They probably wish they were in a magazine too."

"They do. They said they were writing their own magazine stories that would be way better than mine."

"Well, that's okay. Let them. As you get older, you'll learn that whenever you do something that receives positive attention, there will always be people who will have something negative to say, no matter how good your intentions are. They may be jealous; they may disagree with what you're doing; or they may be trying to get attention themselves by criticizing you. That's just the way it is. But you can't let that stop you from doing something you believe is right."

"But I don't want everyone at school to hate me."

"Everyone won't. And if a few of your classmates don't like you simply because you're trying to help other people by sharing your story, then they're not worth being friends with anyway."

I knew my mom was right, but that didn't make dealing with the mean girls any easier. Although I tried not to let their comments bother me, they still did. On the outside, I acted like I didn't care and went about my days as usual, but on the inside I often felt embarrassed and self-conscious. Still, I was determined to do my best to continue to raise awareness of ALD like I knew my dad would have wanted.

The publication of my story came back to haunt me the following year when I ran for vice president of the student council. After the votes were counted and it was announced that I had received the most votes, one of the students who had run against me angrily declared that the only reason I won was because people felt sorry for me because they knew my father had died. And even though I didn't believe that what she said was true, she had been a close friend and her remark cut me to the core.

In the end, I came to realize that sharing my family's story had been worth it, despite the hurtful comments from some of my peers. Most of my classmates were actually very supportive, and many continued to come to me for advice when they were going through difficult times. The Run for ALD was also more successful than ever that year, and we met some amazing ALD families, many of whom have continued to participate in our annual fundraisers to this day.

I also learned two important lessons. First: I would have to develop a thicker skin and face my fear of social rejection if I wanted to continue speaking out and trying to make a difference in the world. Second: If I wanted to stand out, I had to accept that I might not fit in.

CHAPTER TWENTY-ONE

Distressed Genes

By the time I was in sixth grade, I had already known for several years that I had inherited the defective ALD gene (technically the ABCD1 gene) from my dad. In fact, my mom first told me that I was a carrier of ALD when I was around eight or nine. I suppose she would have preferred to withhold this unsettling information from me until I was a little older, but the subject of ALD was common in our household, and there was really no way she could avoid my probing questions. In light of my young age, she explained my carrier status matter-of-factly, in terms that I could understand. She even drew a diagram so I could try to grasp the genetics behind it.

"So, Taylor, Daddy was born with a defective ABCD1 gene, which is located on the X chromosome. I don't really know how to explain chromosomes to you, but they contain genetic information that you inherit from your parents. Males have one X chromosome and one Y chromosome."

My mom wrote the word "Daddy" on the top left corner of a blank piece of paper and placed a large X and a large Y underneath it. Then she took a red magic marker and drew a big dot in the middle of the X. "This dot," she said, "is the defective ABCD1 gene—it causes ALD. This is why Daddy, and why other males with the defective gene, get sick or die . . . Are you following me so far?"

I nodded.

"Females have two X chromosomes; they inherit one from their mother and one from their father." She wrote the word "Mom" next to the word "Daddy" and drew two large Xs underneath it. "These are my X chromosomes. I don't have a defective ABCD1 gene, so there's no red dot on either of my Xs.

"Now," she continued, "Daddy and I had you. You inherited genes from both of us." She wrote the name "Taylor" in the center of the paper. "Since girls have two X chromosomes, you have one of my X chromosomes and Daddy's only X chromosome—the one with the red dot . . . Go ahead and draw your chromosomes under your name."

I understood what my mom was getting at and drew two Xs under my name: one plain X and one with a red dot.

"So you see," she explained, "you have Daddy's red dot—his defective ABCD1 gene—inside your body, but you also have a healthy ABCD1 gene on the X chromosome you inherited from me. The healthy ABCD1 gene sort of cancels out the bad one you got from Daddy. Even though you still carry around the defective gene in your body, you won't get sick from it. That's why girls and women with the defective ABCD1 gene are called carriers."

"What about Matthew? Can he get ALD?"

"No. It's impossible for boys to get ALD from their fathers. Think about it and look at the diagram. A boy has one X chromosome and one Y chromosome. Since I only have X chromosomes, Matthew had to get his Y chromosome from Daddy. And since the ABCD1 gene isn't located on the Y chromosome, Matthew couldn't have inherited ALD."

"What about Tina?"

"Since Daddy is her father, she automatically inherited his X gene, so she's an ALD carrier, like you."

"Does she know?"

"I don't know. But it's her mother's decision if and when to tell her. Not everyone wants their daughters to know that they're carriers until they're older.

So you shouldn't say anything about it to her unless she says something to you about it first.

"Okay, I won't."

"And Taylor, one more thing. Even though you don't have to worry about getting ALD yourself, when you get older and you want to have your own children, you're going to have some difficult decisions to make. Since you're a carrier, if you have a boy, he'll have a 50-50 chance of having the defective gene and getting ALD. If you have a girl, she'll have a 50-50 chance of being a carrier. There are certain medical procedures that can prevent you from passing on the defective gene . . . we don't need to go into that right now. It's just something you will have to be aware of when you grow up."

Learning that I was an ALD carrier didn't scare me or make me upset. Frankly, it really didn't concern me much at all for the next several years—probably because I was so young and my mom had assured me there was no need for me to worry . . . at least not until I was old enough to have children, which seemed a lifetime away.

Over the next few years, however, my mom began to get a little concerned about my carrier status herself when she read online that several studies had determined that up to 20 percent of ALD carriers did, in fact, develop mild to moderate physical symptoms of the disease later in life. So when I was twelve years old, after I began to develop near daily headaches and some unusually high and long-lasting fevers, she made an appointment for me to be evaluated at the Kennedy Krieger Institute by the same doctor who had treated my dad, and to speak to a genetic counselor immediately thereafter.

When the neurologist examined me, however, he quickly dismissed my mom's worries that my symptoms might be related to ALD. I was doing just fine in that respect, he told us, explaining that while some carriers do develop weakness and spasticity of the legs, as well as bladder and bowel dysfunction, it was extremely rare for these symptoms to manifest before adulthood, and uncommon before middle age. He also told us that he was optimistic that effective therapies would be available by the time I reached that age.

Next, my mom and I met with the genetic counselor, a friendly young woman who confirmed what my mom had read online—that around 20 percent of ALD carriers would eventually develop neurological symptoms later in life, but that it was extremely rare for females to develop the deadly cerebral form of the disease that had taken my dad's life. She also detailed various reproductive options that could enable me to have a child free of ALD—procedures such as chorionic villus sampling (where the placenta is biopsied in the first trimester of pregnancy to check for genetic mutations), preimplantation genetic diagnosis performed in conjunction with in vitro fertilization (where eggs from a woman and sperm from a man are retrieved and fertilized to create embryos, which are ultimately biopsied and tested prior to implantation into the woman's uterus), the use of donor eggs, and adoption. Other alternatives might well be available by the time I wanted to have children, she assured me, recommending that I meet with a genetic counselor again prior to starting a family. While this information was a lot to take in, I was relieved to know that I did have options if I decided to have children one day, and that I wouldn't have to risk having a boy who had a 50 percent chance of developing ALD.

I also learned a great deal about my own family history and the inheritance pattern of ALD. The genetic counselor explained that since ALD was an X-linked recessive disease, I was considered an obligate carrier, meaning that the fact that my father had ALD meant that I necessarily carried the ABCD1 gene mutation. We also discussed the extensive history of ALD that ran throughout my dad's side of the family, with my mom providing the information she knew about my family tree. While I already knew about my own uncles and aunt, as well as their children, I learned that my dad had two uncles who had died in childhood of unknown causes (well before ALD was discovered), several aunts who were ALD carriers and who had affected children, and numerous extended family members who had either died from, were affected with, or carried the disease. It was frightening to realize how a genetic disease could ravage an entire family, particularly a disease as deadly as ALD.

I will always be grateful to my mom for informing me that I was an ALD carrier and arranging for me to meet with a genetic counselor when I was young. Although all children are different, for me, learning about my carrier status as a pre-teen was far less traumatic and life-altering than it would have been had I found out later on. While it was certainly a little unnerving to realize that I had the same defective gene in my body that took my father's life, the fact that my childbearing years were still so far away allowed me plenty of time to process what I had learned and come to terms with it. And while I understood that there was a chance that I would develop mild symptoms, that too was well in the future—probably four or five decades away. I suppose that at the time, I was just so relieved that I wouldn't develop the deadly, cerebral form of ALD that afflicted so many boys born with the defective gene that my prognosis seemed like a blessing.

CHAPTER TWENTY-TWO

Telling My Story

The first boy I ever met who was affected by ALD was an eleven-year-old named Matthew. He shared the same name and was the same age as my brother. But while my brother spent most of his time attending school, playing video games with his friends, and competing in baseball and basketball, this Matthew was confined to a hospital bed in his parents' home, unable to speak, see, or take care of his own basic needs. My mom had met his parents at a fundraiser that had been organized to assist with his medical care, and when she learned that they lived only a few towns away, she quickly arranged to visit. I begged her to let me come too.

During the twenty-minute car ride to Matthew's house, my mom told me what she had learned from his parents. Matthew had begun having difficulty in school at the age of seven, and like many boys with ALD, he was misdiagnosed with attention-deficit/hyperactivity disorder. His symptoms continued to worsen, and he began to have vision problems. By the time Matthew was finally diagnosed with ALD, it was too late for a bone marrow transplant. There was nothing that could be done to save him.

"Are you sure you're going to be able to handle this?" my mom asked me. "It will probably bring back a lot of memories of your dad."

"I'm sure," I insisted. "I want to be there for Matthew."

When we finally arrived and walked up to the door, we were greeted by his parents—two of the kindest and most loving people you could ever imagine. Pictures of Matthew from the days when he was young and healthy adorned their home. There was Matthew swinging a baseball bat; Matthew riding his bicycle; Matthew wearing a firefighter's uniform. He was a beautiful boy with an infectious smile. He was his parents' pride and joy—their only child.

Now, Matthew quietly lay in a bed in the family room, most of his physical and cognitive abilities stripped away. I knew he couldn't see me, but when I took his hand I could tell that he knew I was there. There wasn't much I could do but talk to him and hope he understood how much I cared. Matthew was still fighting hard, his mom told us. His entire town was rooting for him, and he was holding strong.

Matthew and his family became an important part of my life. I visited as often as I could, and his parents and relatives became regular fixtures at the annual Run for ALD, always supporting our efforts to raise money to find a cure. Knowing Matthew and witnessing his brave battle with ALD inspired me to redouble my efforts and devote my time and energy to what would prove to be my most significant endeavor to date: convincing my home state of New Jersey to screen newborns for ALD.

It was hard to believe that April 29, 2012, marked our Eleventh Annual Run for ALD. By this time, I was in eighth grade. As I had every year in the past, I addressed the large crowd of participants and supporters who had gathered by the end of the event, telling them about my dad's battle with ALD and the need for more research so that one day there would be a cure for this horrific disease. I also proudly announced that with their help, over the past eleven years we had donated more than $150,000 to the Kennedy Krieger Institute to help fund these research efforts.

My mom and I also learned some exciting news at the run: the Kennedy Krieger Institute had recently developed a test whereby newborn babies could be screened for ALD. This was an extremely significant accomplishment, as it would enable boys with the defective gene to be identified before they developed symptoms; in turn, these boys could undergo a timely bone marrow or stem cell transplant and have a good chance of surviving ALD. In fact, recent studies showed that the success rate of early transplants for ALD approached 90 percent.

My mom told me that she knew infants were typically screened for a number of diseases immediately after they were born, but she didn't know much else about newborn screening, so over the next several weeks she did some research. We learned that each individual state had its own newborn screening program through which babies born within its borders were tested for a number of potentially fatal or disabling disorders that are treatable but not apparent at birth. The goal of all of these screening programs was to diagnose infants in time for them to receive effective treatment. Nationwide, millions of babies were routinely screened for certain genetic and congenital disorders every year before they left the hospital by testing a few drops of blood taken from the heel. The conditions for which a particular infant was screened, however, depended upon the state in which he or she was born. While every state's newborn screening panel included at least twenty-nine conditions, some states screened for more than fifty disorders. This variation between different states existed as the result of a number of factors, including the amount of funding a state had for its newborn screening program, the state's particular laws and policies, and the availability of treatment for each condition. Our home state of New Jersey had a very comprehensive newborn screening program, testing infants for fifty-four different conditions.

My mom told me that she thought there might be something we could do to help get the newly developed newborn screening test for ALD implemented in New Jersey, and perhaps across the country. "I'm not really sure how we go about it though," she told me one evening as she looked up from her computer. "I think there has to be a law directing the Department of Health to start screening for ALD."

"So how do we get a law like that?" I asked.

"That's a good question. Every town in our state has representatives in the legislature. In New Jersey, there are senators and members of the assembly. One of these representatives would have to draft a bill requiring ALD newborn screening, and then they all vote on it. If a majority votes in favor of the bill, the legislature sends it to the governor of New Jersey, who has to decide whether or not to sign the bill into law."

"So how do we get one of the representatives to write a bill?"

"I don't know, since I don't know any of them personally. If you want to try to help, maybe you could write a letter to the legislators telling your story, like you did for the magazine. You could tell them about the new screening test and ask them to introduce a newborn screening bill."

"Do you think that would work?"

"It's the only thing I can think of right now. And I think a letter would be good, especially coming from you. You've always had positive responses whenever you talk about ALD. And how could they say no when screening for ALD could save the lives of so many boys born in New Jersey?"

I understood that it was a longshot, but the past few years had shown me the power inherent in telling my story and had proven that I had the potential to make a difference. I decided to write to the president of the New Jersey Senate and set to work on my letter.

Dear Senator, I began.

My name is Taylor Kane. I am thirteen years old, and I live in Mount Laurel. I am writing to ask you to introduce a bill that would require New Jersey to screen all newborns for adrenoleukodystrophy (ALD). Could you please read my story so you understand how important this is, and how many lives would be saved if New Jersey screened newborns for ALD?

I continued on, telling the senator about ALD and how my dad passed away from the disease when I was five years old. I wrote about the newborn screening test that had been developed by the Kennedy Krieger Institute and how it could benefit boys like my new friend, Matthew, whom I visited from time to time.

By the time [Matthew's] parents found out he had ALD, I explained in my letter, *it was too late for him to be saved. Matthew is very sick now, and hasn't been able to walk or talk in a few years. He probably will not live much longer. If New Jersey requires newborn screening for ALD, boys like Matthew will have a good chance of being cured.*

I told the senator that if he needed more information about the screening test, my mom and I could meet with him.

Take it from me, I wrote, *the girl who has had a firsthand experience of what it's like to lose a family member. It hurts. If I could help save someone's life, even if it's just one, I know my dad would be proud. If New Jersey screens newborns for ALD, I know we can save lives.*

After I finished the letter and signed my name, I attached a copy of the magazine article I had written, addressed an envelope, and gave it to my mom to take to the post office. I had no idea if or when I would receive a response.

Two months later, just after the fourth of July, I was outside playing in our next-door neighbor's backyard when my mom called out for me to come home. When I got there, she handed me an envelope. It was addressed to me.

"It's from the senator's office," my mom said in an excited voice. "Go ahead and open it."

I carefully opened the envelope, took out the letter, and read it to myself. I was prepared to read a form letter from a staff member containing boilerplate language telling me that the senator would take my suggestion under advisement. But as I kept reading, my eyes widened and my heart skipped a beat.

"Mom!" I cried as I got to the middle of the letter. "The senator says he has introduced Senate Bill 2137, which will provide for the screening of newborns for ALD!"

"Oh my God, I can't believe it!" she exclaimed. "That's fantastic. I told you you could do it . . . Your dad would be so proud of you."

"So they have to vote on it now, right? How long do you think that will take?"

"I have no idea what comes next. I guess we'll just have to wait and see if we hear anything else."

We didn't have to wait too long. In early September, just after I had started my freshman year of high school, my mom received a telephone call asking if I could testify before the New Jersey Senate Health Committee in support of the bill. She knew I would be thrilled and quickly accepted the invitation for me. When she told me about it later that day, I was extremely excited and immediately got to work on what I wanted to tell the committee. I didn't have much time to prepare, as the hearing was scheduled for the following week.

When the day of the hearing arrived the following week, my mom picked me up from school early, and I put on one of my nicest dresses. After a thirty-minute drive, we arrived at the golden-domed capitol building in Trenton. The large room where the hearing was being held was filled with people, and we sat down in the back next to Matthew's mother and the mayor of his hometown, who had come to support me. We waited for an hour or two, listening to other people testify, both in support of and against a number of other bills that were before the committee. Finally, S-2137 was called. It was my turn.

As I walked up to the front table to sit down in front of the microphone, I looked around and breathed a sigh of relief to see that I was the only one testifying. (I had been a little worried that someone might come up to the front to testify against the newborn screening bill after what I had seen happen with some of the other bills.) I suddenly felt very calm and was determined to do my best. After introducing myself to the senators, I took a deep breath and read the statement I had prepared, hitting many of the same points as I had in my letter to the senate president, but in greater detail. I concluded my statement by imploring the health committee to approve the bill:

"Mr. Chairman and Committee members, I've been working to raise awareness of ALD in my dad's memory ever since third grade. I've also done everything I can to raise money for ALD research, from selling lemonade to volunteering at the annual 5k Run for ALD in Pennsauken. Now, there is finally a way to save boys and men from this horrible disease. Please—for the sake of my dad, boys like Matthew . . . and all of the other families in New Jersey who are or may be affected by ALD—approve this bill so that ALD will be added to New Jersey's current newborn screening panel."

After I was finished, the chairman thanked me for my testimony and jokingly agreed to sign a note excusing me for missing school that afternoon.

Just as the committee was about to vote, a woman entered the hearing room and said she wanted to testify against the bill. My heart sank. My worst fear had come true. I couldn't even imagine what she was going to say.

Fortunately, she was told that she had come in too late and that she would have to submit her written statement for the record. I let out a sigh of relief.

The chairman instructed the committee to take a vote. To my amazement, every senator on the panel voted yes! The bill had made it out of the Senate Health Committee and would be going on to the full Senate!

The following month, I heard that Governor Chris Christie was coming to my hometown for a town hall meeting. Although I wasn't overly interested in politics at the time, I knew that the newborn screening bill would likely land on his desk in the near future, and that he would ultimately have to decide whether or not to sign it into law.

"Do you think we can go to the town hall meeting?" I asked my mom. "I want to meet Governor Christie and talk to him about the ALD newborn screening bill. It's after school, so I wouldn't have to miss any class time."

My mom smiled. "Taylor, there will be so many people at that meeting, you'll never get to talk to him personally. He'll be standing up at the front speaking in front of a huge crowd."

"Well, people get to ask questions at town hall meetings. I can bring it up by asking him a question."

My mom shook her head. "He probably won't take that many questions . . . but if you really want to go, I can leave work early and take you, though I wouldn't count on being called on."

Despite what my mom said, I was convinced that I would get a chance to speak to Governor Christie about the newborn screening bill if I went to the town hall meeting. After all, I had been lucky so far in my advocacy efforts. I knew I wouldn't have enough time to tell the governor everything I wanted to about ALD and the importance of newborn screening, so I compiled all of the information I had, including a copy of my magazine article and my letter to the senate president, as well as the bills that had been introduced in the senate and assembly, and put them in a binder. I was determined to find a way to get this information to him so that he could understand how important it was that he sign the bill into law.

On the afternoon of October 11, 2012, when we pulled into the parking lot of the Burlington County YMCA, I was a little disheartened to see an incredibly long line of people wrapped around the building waiting to get inside for the town hall meeting.

"I told you there would be a lot of people," my mom said, "but I didn't expect there to be this many. We might not even get in."

After standing in the long line for ten minutes or so, my mom spotted the mayor who had come to the state house to support me when I testified before the health committee. He waved us over and told my mom that he had a few reserved seats for guests that were still empty if we wanted to use them. My mom didn't hesitate to accept his offer, and we followed the mayor directly into the huge indoor arena where the governor would be speaking. He showed us to our seats, which were only a few rows from the floor. Looking around at the nearly full arena, I realized how lucky we were to get a seat this close to the front. Still, there were hundreds of people around us, with even more filing in to sit in the upper gallery. I placed the folder I had prepared for the governor on my lap and read over the questions I had written down on a separate sheet of paper.

When the governor came out, I immediately recognized him from seeing him on television. He spoke for a while, then began calling on people in the audience who were raising their hands to ask him questions. He selected several people who asked him about taxes and sick leave for government workers and things of that nature. After a while, I began to get a little nervous because he hadn't even looked in my direction, but suddenly he turned my way and I knew I had a chance. I raised my hand and caught his eye. The governor pointed at me. I quickly stood up and was handed a microphone.

"Governor Christie," I began, "my father died from a rare disease called adrenoleukodystrophy, and I have two questions. I know you haven't seen this bill yet, but how do you feel about expanding New Jersey's current newborn screening panel?"

The governor responded by stating that he had expanded New Jersey's newborn screening panel twice already, and that if the evidence supported expanding it for ALD, he would likely be in favor of it.

"When a bill comes to you from the senate," I asked him, "do you consider the information that regular New Jersey citizens give you, and if you do, could you look at this information I prepared?"

"Sure," he said and waved for me to hand my folder to him.

"I did this instead of doing my homework," I admitted as I handed him the folder.

The governor laughed and the audience applauded, then he leafed through the folder and noted its contents, seemingly impressed with all of the information I had included.

"Do you want a job on my staff?" he said jokingly. After the laughter died down, he told me he would read the material in the car on his ride home.

When I took my seat, my mom whispered to me that I had done a good job and that she couldn't believe that the governor had actually called on me. I couldn't believe it either. The rest of the town hall meeting went by in a blur, and my heart was pounding so loudly in my ears that I could hardly hear the rest of the questions and the governor's responses. When the town hall meeting was over, four or five different reporters stopped me and asked me questions about ALD and the newborn screening bill. A local college admissions officer even approached me and told me there would be a scholarship waiting if I decided to apply to the college he represented. (My mom and I laughed about this later—after all, I had just asked a few simple questions.) It took us a while to get out of the building, but when we did I was excited and happy. I hoped that the governor would keep his promise.

Over the next nine months, the ALD newborn screening bill bounced back and forth between various senate committees. In the assembly, three different assemblymen—including one who represented my hometown district—cosponsored an identical version of the bill. After passing both legislative bodies, the bill finally made it to Governor Christie the following August. And although I don't know for sure whether he actually read the information I had given him at the town hall meeting, on August 7, 2013, the governor signed the bill into law, making New Jersey the third state in the nation to enact an ALD newborn screening law.

I couldn't have been happier, knowing that once this law was implemented, it would undoubtedly save the lives of many boys born in New Jersey who would have otherwise been diagnosed too late. I marveled at the fact that this had all come about by me simply writing a letter to a state senator telling my story. Who would have thought that people—influential ones like lawmakers and governors—would actually listen to an ordinary thirteen year old? The realization that someone like me could make a significant, positive difference in the world without being wealthy, having political connections, or even being old enough to drive, opened up a world of possibilities. It was a lesson that I knew I had to share.

CHAPTER TWENTY-THREE

The Power of Volunteering

Even before I began high school, I was determined to be an "official volunteer" for a charitable organization, in addition to Run for ALD, where I could help people in some way. I would have been happy doing anything—from folding envelopes to raking leaves—but it was extremely difficult to find an organization that would take me on because of my age. My mom regularly searched for volunteer opportunities online, but most had a minimum age requirement of sixteen. I applied anyway. The few organizations that responded said I was still too young.

When I was fourteen, a local hospice agreed to interview me for a volunteer position, despite my age. I was thrilled. Volunteering at a hospice was something I had always wanted to do, as I had been so close with the hospice nurses who had cared for my dad, and I never forgot their kindness and dedication.

When I went in for the interview, I sat at a large conference room table while three volunteer coordinators asked me questions. I told them why I wanted to be a volunteer and how important it was to me to give back to an organization like the one that had helped my family so much when my dad was sick. I guess they could tell how sincere I was because they quickly agreed to allow me to volunteer and told me that they would find special tasks for me to do. Since I had told them I was involved in musical theater and they could tell I was not shy, they offered me the opportunity to sing and speak at their biannual memorial services, which were held to honor those who had passed away. I quickly agreed.

The volunteer coordinators also mentioned that they would like me to attend their summer bereavement camp for children who had lost a loved one. Although I would still be too young to be a junior counselor that coming summer, they asked me to attend as if I were a camper and report back to them afterward about which activities I felt were most effective and whether I had any recommendations for improving the program. If all went well, they assured me I could be a junior counselor the next summer.

I was very grateful for this new opportunity, and proud that I was now an actual volunteer. I took my duties very seriously and became a regular soloist and speaker at the hospice's memorial services—something I continued doing until I went away to college. I always carefully chose the songs I sang at a service, trying to find something appropriate and meaningful like "Somewhere Over the Rainbow" or "Wind Beneath My Wings." Often, I was accompanied by a harpist. At the end of the memorial service, when audience members were instructed that they could come up to the front and say a few words about the loved one they had lost, I often spoke first, telling those gathered about my dad and what I had learned from losing him. This would usually break the ice and encourage others to come up and share their stories.

I also attended the hospice's summer bereavement camp, first as a participant-observer, and then as a junior counselor. Volunteering as a junior counselor was undoubtedly one of the most poignant and fulfilling experiences I've ever had. I watched as young children who had lost a parent or sibling bonded with other children who had undergone a similar tragedy. I listened to each one of them talk about how their loved one had died—whether it be suddenly and unexpectedly, as the result of a horrific accident or massive heart attack, or after a long and debilitating illness. Each child grieved in his or her own way—some were outwardly tearful and distraught, others angry and resentful, still others quiet and detached. I saw their pain and, remembering how I felt in the years after my dad's death, did my best to comfort them and assure them that they would be okay. Many of these children would repeatedly hug me or grasp tightly onto my hand, not wanting to let go. They knew that I had once been in their shoes and could see that I had not only survived, but that I had thrived.

Serving as a counselor at this summer camp had a huge impact on my life. It reinforced what I had learned in the years immediately following my father's death—that for children, connecting with peers who personally understand their struggles can be transformative, allowing them to see that they are not alone and helping them to heal. Guiding and forming relationships with these amazing children helped me as much as it helped them.

As luck would have it, several other volunteer opportunities opened up to me shortly after I began high school, and I threw myself into these as well. The first was working with dementia and Alzheimer's patients at an assisted living facility in the town adjacent to my own. Once or twice a week, I spent several hours pushing a supply cart from room to room, offering the residents a variety of useful items, such as hair brushes, books, and snacks. My friends Emily and Craig agreed to volunteer with me, and together we entertained the residents in the common area, leading them in playing trivia games and bingo. Although a few of the residents clearly enjoyed the games a great deal, most were unable to actually participate and just watched the fun from their wheelchairs. As part of our duties, my friends and I also facilitated parties and events, and wheeled the residents to other parts of the building for meals or medical appointments.

Even though it was very rare that a resident remembered us the next time we returned for our rounds, even when it was only a few days later, the lack of recognition didn't deter us. We all still felt like we were doing something important and worthwhile. Helping these residents was particularly meaningful to me personally, since I still remembered what it was like when my dad experienced episodes of dementia. In a strange way, the assisted living facility felt like home.

Beginning in my sophomore year of high school, I was also fortunate to have the opportunity to serve as a volunteer intern for then-Assemblyman (now State Senator) Troy Singleton, who was my district's representative in the New Jersey legislature. He was also one of the assemblymen who had cosponsored the ALD newborn screening bill the previous year. The internship opportunity came about shortly after I wrote to Assemblyman Singleton to seek his help in getting New Jersey to actually implement the law and begin screening newborns for ALD. (The state's position was that certain conditions in the law had not yet been satisfied and that it would not begin screening until these conditions were met.)

After he received my letter, Assemblyman Singleton invited my mom and me to his office to discuss the newborn screening situation. Although it was the first time I had met him in person, at the close of our meeting, Troy—as he had insisted we call him— asked me if I wanted to come to his office a few days each week after school and serve as his intern. Of course, I jumped at the opportunity. I had become much more knowledgeable about politics by that point, and although I certainly had no aspirations of becoming a politician myself, I was intrigued by the chance to learn more about the legislative process and to see democracy in action.

Although some of my days at Troy's office were spent performing clerical duties, I also spent a good amount of time researching interesting issues and policy initiatives and interacting with constituents. Even better was the time I got to spend with Troy and his team at community events. There were local fundraisers and health fairs and parades and family fun days—the list went on and on. Troy never stopped working for the betterment of the community or advocating for his constituents. Still, despite his busy schedule, he always made time for anyone who wanted to talk, or to support a worthy cause. He was gregarious, kind-hearted, and fun, and always made me feel like a valued member of his team.

The lessons I learned in the two and a half years I spent as an intern in Troy's office were invaluable. Watching him work and seeing the amount of energy and dedication he put into everything he did, inspired me to do the same in my own life. Troy Singleton taught me what it meant to be a true public servant. I have always considered myself very lucky to have had such an incredible mentor.

Admittedly, I did spend an extensive amount of time volunteering during my high school years, and as a result, some people (mostly my friends' parents) seemed to consider me some sort of paragon of virtue. I can assure you that I was not. I was a typical teenage girl—obsessed with my cell phone, continually complaining that I didn't have enough clothes, binge-watching Netflix, and often staying out past my curfew to attend parties (many of which my mom definitely would not have approved of). There was regular drama with my friends, and my inability to control my temper when faced with a perceived injustice often led to fierce battles with my mom and, embarrassingly, even a few teachers who I felt were treating the class (or me) unfairly. But engaging in community service and helping other people always brought me back to earth. It made me see that many of the things I craved, like being able to buy designer clothes and having hordes of Instagram followers, were really not that important, especially when there were so many people hurting and in need.

I learned so many things through my volunteer experiences—compassion, teamwork, organizational and leadership skills, public speaking, and an appreciation for people of all ages, backgrounds, and circumstances—that have benefited me in every aspect of my life. I also found a sense of joy and happiness that I couldn't seem to find anywhere else, no matter how hard I searched. Although I originally began volunteering to emulate my dad and carry on his legacy, in the end it was something I did for me.

CHAPTER TWENTY-FOUR

Anyone Can Be a Hero

———————————

The high school I attended was relatively large, with nearly five hundred students in my graduating class alone. One of the best things about my school was the fact it was less than a quarter mile from my home. But because I either had to walk down a busy highway or cut through a dense area of woods and climb over a wire fence to get there, my mom usually dropped me off in the morning on her way to work. This allowed me to sleep as late as possible and leave the house every morning at 7:26 a.m., just four minutes before the start of homeroom. Since I'm definitely not a morning person, this was an ideal situation.

At the beginning of my freshman year, I envisioned myself becoming an athlete and decided to try out for the volleyball team. Despite being in relatively good shape (or so I thought), I could barely make it through the rigorous preseason workouts, and the intense running drills left me doubled over and gasping for breath. After a few days, the writing was on the wall so to speak, and I withdrew from volleyball before tryouts even began.

Notwithstanding this setback, my determination to play a sport persisted, and I decided to try out for the much less competitive freshman lacrosse team. Although I had never played lacrosse before, rumor had it that everyone who tried out made the team. Fortunately for me the rumor was true, and I ended up on the freshman team. Although I had fun, I wasn't very good and spent most of my time sitting on the bench. (I did score one goal during the season—a small but personally memorable accomplishment.) It didn't take me long to realize that I was simply not cut out for competitive sports. So, it was back to what I was more comfortable with: serving as a class officer and participating in my school's community service clubs.

I ran for—and was elected—class secretary my freshman year, joined the Community Service Club, the Buddies Club, and the Students Against Destructive Decisions Club, and was selected to serve on the principal's leadership council. While I was initially eager to be involved in all of these activities, it wasn't long before I became a bit disenchanted. Sure, we cut out decorations to hang in the hallways for pep rallies, listened to speakers from various nonprofit organizations, and spent a lot of time making crafts for a variety of worthwhile causes, but I didn't feel the sense of satisfaction that I got from my extracurricular volunteer experiences. Most of the other students didn't appear to be too enthusiastic either; in fact, it seemed to me that many showed up at the after-school club meetings simply because they needed community service hours on their college resumes, or for the pizza that was often provided as an enticement to increase club attendance. I expressed my frustration to my mom one night over dinner around the middle of my freshman year.

"Mom, being class secretary is pretty much a joke. I don't take minutes of meetings, make any decisions, or do anything that a real secretary would do. The other class officers and I mostly just spend hours upon hours decorating the hallways. I've cut so many pieces of construction paper, I think I have permanent scissor marks on my hand. I feel like I'm back in kindergarten."

My mom shook her head, acknowledging my disappointment.

"And in most of the community service clubs," I continued, "we don't really do that much actual community service. The students don't have any say in who we help or what activities we do. I wish the clubs could be more interactive and that students were more involved in the planning process instead of just mindlessly following directions. And I also think kids would be a lot more interested in volunteering if they got to meet some of the people they're helping and see how they're making a difference in their lives. It seems like we spend hours working to raise money or making crafts for some cause, but hardly ever actually get to see the results or the impact of what we've done."

"That's a good point," my mom agreed. "I definitely think kids are much more likely to enjoy volunteering and community service if they have a personal connection with the particular cause or person they're trying to help. And seeing tangible results is important too. But it is school. There's only so much they can do. Maybe you could make some suggestions to the teachers who run the community service clubs about ways you think they could be improved."

"I was actually thinking about starting my own school club," I told my mom. "In fact, I already looked up how to do it on the school website. It's not that hard."

"Well, that's a nice idea, but it would take a lot of time and effort on your part. You're already doing so much outside of school, and you do have to keep up your grades so you can get into a good college."

"I know. I still want to try."

I spent the next month or two mulling over various ideas and decided to model my club after a social media helping network called Wish Upon a Hero, which connected people in need (people with a wish) with people who wanted to help (the heroes). I drafted guidelines for my club proposal which provided that the students, rather than a teacher, would (1) collectively select an individual in the local community to help; (2) decide exactly how to help that person—whether through a fundraiser or direct action; (3) plan the fundraiser or activity and promote it over social media; and (4) witness the granting of the wish to the recipient, so they could experience first-hand the joy of having helped someone in need. At the suggestion of the Wish Upon a Hero Network, I called the club "Hero Club" and was determined that it would prove to every student that by simply taking the time and making the effort to help another person, he or she could be a hero.

The school rules required that every club have a teacher as an advisor. I decided to ask my business teacher, who was new to the school and seemed like a very caring person, if he would take on this role. After I explained my vision to him, he immediately accepted. Next, I collected the ten student signatures required to start a new club and presented my proposal to the athletics and activities director. Then, I waited to find out whether Hero Club would be approved as a sanctioned school club.

A few weeks later, Hero Club was approved. Since my freshman year was nearly over by this point, Hero Club would officially start in the fall of my sophomore year. Although I knew the idea behind the club was a good one, I was a little (actually a lot) worried that Hero Club would be ridiculed and that the backlash I faced in middle school would resurface. I was also afraid no one would join.

I needn't have worried. Over the next three years, Hero Club quickly became one of the most popular and successful clubs in my high school, with more than one hundred and fifty active members by the time I was a senior. Over that time period, the club granted twenty-five wishes for people in need in both our local community and around the country. The club was so well regarded, in fact, that its accomplishments were portrayed in several newspaper and magazine articles. The enthusiasm of the many students who participated in Hero Club was incredible to behold.

One of the first wishes Hero Club granted involved an elderly woman named Alice who lived a few towns away, and who was paralyzed from the waist down. We learned about Alice from one of our own Hero Club members whose father was a doctor and who was aware of her situation. Alice lived alone and was in desperate need of a hospital bed with an arm trapeze lift so that she could pull herself up and shift around in her bed, both to enable her to reach for personal care items and to prevent bedsores. Sadly, while Medicare had agreed to pay 80 percent of the bed's cost, Alice could not afford the other 20 percent.

Club members quickly agreed that we would do whatever we could to raise enough money for Alice to get her hospital bed. We decided on something simple and fun—a scratch card fundraiser—where every club member could participate by asking family, friends, and acquaintances to scratch off a few circles and then donate the amounts revealed.

We got to work and within a few weeks had cumulatively raised more than enough to pay for Alice's hospital bed. I called the medical supply company and arranged to pay the copay and have the bed delivered to Alice's home the following week.

On the night before the bed was scheduled to be delivered, I called Alice and asked her if I could bring two other Hero Club officers to her home the next day to help set up the bed. She happily agreed.

My mom drove us all to Alice's tiny home the following afternoon after school. When we arrived at the address Alice had provided to us, we noticed that the front door was slightly ajar and stepped inside the poorly lit living room to find Alice lying on a small mattress on the floor. Her tiny frame was covered by a blanket; her head was propped up by a thick pillow. She looked so frail, and as she acknowledged our presence with her eyes, it was clear that she couldn't even prop herself up on the mattress. I had to bite my lip to keep myself from crying at the thought that she had lived alone like this—confined to a mattress on the floor—for several years. But Alice didn't seem to feel sorry for herself.

"I'm so glad to meet all of you," she said with a bright smile. "I can't thank you enough for what you've done for me. The medical supply company just left. They set up the new bed in the other room." She turned her head to the right, and following her gaze, we saw a shiny new hospital bed standing in the next room over.

"Does it have the arm trapeze you needed?" I asked.

"It's perfect," Alice said. "You see, it's not just that I can't get out of bed, I can't even sit up by myself or move from side to side without help. My son comes over most days after he's done working, and he helps me move around a bit and take care of my personal needs." She motioned us to come closer to her. We crouched down on the floor at the end of her mattress.

"Once I'm in the new bed," she told us, "I'll be able to use the arm trapeze to pull myself up into a seated position, and I'll be able to reach for things by myself . . . I can't tell you how much this means to me."

We all made our way over to the head of the mattress and gave Alice a hug.

"We have something else for you," I said, holding up an envelope. "It's a check for $150. It's what was left over from our fundraiser after we paid for the hospital bed."

Alice's eyes widened with surprise and gratitude. "You are angels," she said. "Thank you so very much."

It struck me then how little it actually took to make someone's life better, and how sad it was that no one had done it sooner.

Before we left, we took some pictures so the rest of the Hero Club members could see Alice and her new hospital bed for themselves. Alice also made us promise to tell them all how much she appreciated what they had done to help her.

A week later, the Hero Club advisor gave me an envelope addressed to Hero Club that had been delivered to our school. Inside was a card was from Alice, thanking us again, and telling us that she was sitting up in her hospital bed, enjoying reading a book for the first time in a very long time. It felt good to know that we had made a difference.

There were other memorable wish grants too. One year, we organized a bowling fundraiser at nearby Laurel Lanes that we called the Hero Bowl, and raised more than $4,000 for two different students in our school district who were fighting cancer.

In the fall of my junior year, we traveled to a nearby farm where Hero Club members collectively picked 162 pounds of corn and sweet potatoes, which we donated to a community food pantry. This event—the Hero Harvest—was one of our most popular activities, and probably the most fun.

And at the end of my senior year, I met a man named David at a local mall trying to sell a children's book he had published about his service dog, Lucky. After learning that David was an alumni of our high school who was not only a recovering addict, but who had survived a suicide attempt, I invited him to speak at a Hero Club meeting about the lessons he had learned during his life. At the meeting, David eloquently told us about his road to recovery from depression, anxiety, and drug abuse, and how his passion for writing children's books kept him going and gave him something to live for. At the end of the meeting, we presented David with a check for one hundred dollars to help finance the publishing of his third children's book.

There were many more wishes granted during my three years as Hero Club president, each unique, special, and meaningful in its own way. Students collectively chose not only who we helped, but how we helped, then planned and organized all of the club's fundraisers and activities. To the greatest extent possible, the students also shared in the granting of the wish: a donation might be presented to the recipient at an after-school club meeting, or delivered personally by students, with photos taken to share with the rest of the club members. The wish grant was the culmination of our efforts—the "feel good" part of the experience—and we wanted every student to have the opportunity to feel like they had made the world a little better for someone else. Getting to see the grateful smile on the face of the wish recipient helped to accomplish that.

Every year membership in Hero Club increased exponentially. It became the "cool" club to join—something unique in itself since volunteering isn't always something that lends itself to popularity among teenagers.

Because I personally spent so much time and effort in trying to establish Hero Club and ensure that it was successful, I was a little worried about what would happen to it once I graduated high school. Would a new group of students continue to work as hard? Would they have the same drive and initiative to continue its mission?

Three years later, I am happy to report that Hero Club is still going as strong as ever, perhaps even stronger. Its membership is enormous. The club's ongoing success is a testament to the fact that kids—even surly teenagers—really do want to help others and make the world a better place. They just need the right vehicle to encourage them to view an unfortunate or unjust situation as an opportunity to help, and to show them that they really do have the ability to make a difference.

Studies abound demonstrating that volunteering can be life-changing for kids. I certainly can attest to that. I've also had friends tell me about service projects they've taken on or philanthropic careers they are pursuing as a result of having gained the confidence to do so after participating in Hero Club.

I truly believe that kids would be happier and the world would be a better place if every school in the country had its own Hero Club.

CHAPTER TWENTY-FIVE

Reaching Out

Shortly after I began my junior year of high school, I began to feel like something was seriously wrong with me, both physically and mentally. The year had begun relatively smoothly. I enjoyed my teachers and classes and was thrilled to spend another year as president of Hero Club. But as the weeks went on, I started experiencing some scary and unsettling symptoms—daily headaches and nausea, dizziness, tremors, and an overarching feeling that something bad was going to happen to me or my family.

At first, I tried to ignore these symptoms. I just didn't have time to deal with them; I had far too much to do between managing my rigorous course load, leading Hero Club, interning and volunteering outside of school, and studying for the upcoming SATs. I took Advil every four to six hours to manage my headaches and stopped drinking as much caffeine to help with my near-constant shaking. Unfortunately, my symptoms weren't going away.

Still, I continued to keep what I was experiencing to myself. *I have to fight through this*, I thought. *Surely I'll get over whatever it is and be back to normal soon.*

As the school year continued on, my symptoms didn't get any better. I also began to experience new symptoms, including an inability to focus, shortness of breath, and constant lethargy. I knew I had to go to a doctor, but I was reluctant to tell my mom about all of my problems because I didn't want to disappoint or worry her. I tried to create an elevator pitch in my head . . . "Hey, Mom, so

I've been shaking so much that I can hardly hold a pencil. I think something's wrong with me." Or, "Hi, Mom! How was your day? Mine was good, other than the fact that I can't focus on anything and I feel like I can't breathe!"

On a Sunday afternoon, I approached my mom in her home office and prepared to present my symptoms as if I were a doctor explaining a patient's diagnosis. Instead, when I met her eyes I burst into tears.

Later that week, my mom took me to our family doctor who referred me to get blood work to test for mono, anemia, Lyme disease, and various other maladies. A few days later, the doctor invited my mom and me back to her office to discuss the results.

"Taylor," she said, "all of your blood work came back negative. Based upon these results, and given the symptoms you described, I'm pretty sure that what you've been experiencing is anxiety."

Honestly, I wasn't surprised. I remembered having some of these feelings and symptoms when I was younger, but deep down was hoping they were caused by something else. Something where I could simply take a pill every day and feel like myself again.

The doctor turned to my mom. "I think it would be helpful if Taylor saw a therapist. I could recommend one if you'd like."

I began seeing a therapist two weeks later. After several sessions, she diagnosed me with generalized anxiety disorder and major depressive disorder and recommended that I start taking medication to help with the symptoms.

I followed her instructions. At first, I was embarrassed about my diagnosis. Sure, I knew it was normal to feel nervous and sad sometimes, but it was hard to wrap my head around the fact that I had a true mental health condition. *How could this happen to me?* I asked myself. *I know my life hasn't always been easy, but I felt like I was doing so well. Am I doomed to feel this way forever? What will people think if they find out?*

I felt trapped inside my own head. I was incredibly scared that if the people in my life found out about my anxiety and depression, it would be impossible for them to think of me the same way. I truly believed that all the work I had to put into establishing myself as a leader in my school and community had gone to waste. I was lost.

I continued to see my therapist, Karrie, weekly, and slowly some of my fears and worries abated. She taught me ways to calm my nerves and put the negative thoughts aside and made me feel more hopeful for the future.

After my diagnosis, I thought a lot about what the causes of my anxiety might be. To be sure, I was going through an incredibly stressful time in my life. I was taking a number of AP courses, studying daily for the SATs, and looking at colleges . . . but so were many other of my classmates. Why could they handle the stress while I couldn't?

I also wondered if the anxiety was a residual feeling from losing my dad, one that would never completely go away. Maybe I would always worry that something bad was going to happen and would therefore experience endless shaking and other physical side effects. I found this prospect extremely unsettling.

There was something else too. Over the course of the last few months, I found myself increasingly concerned about what being a genetic carrier of ALD meant for my future. Yes, I was only sixteen years old and a lifetime away from having children, but the thought that somehow my carrier status would negatively impact my life was always in the back of my mind. In addition, more recent studies of female ALD carriers had shown that more than 80 percent would go on to experience physical manifestations of the disease at some point in their lives, including progressive stiffness, weakness, and spasticity of the legs; difficulty walking and balancing; and bladder and bowel incontinence. This was a terrifying revelation, as most prior studies had estimated that only 20 percent of female carriers would be physically affected by the disease.

For the first time in my life, the fact that I was an ALD carrier seriously worried me. While I do not believe it was a direct cause of my anxiety and depression, I do believe it played a role. The thought of telling future romantic partners that I was a carrier of a deadly disease that I could pass on to my children and that could physically affect me when I got older made me incredibly apprehensive. I thought, *When is the right time to tell someone? Will being a carrier damage my prospect for a happy long-term relationship?*

I didn't know where to turn or with whom to talk about my feelings. My close friends knew I was a carrier, but since they were not in my shoes, I knew it would be difficult for them to understand my distress. I didn't even feel completely comfortable discussing these issues with my mom, despite her familiarity with ALD. I longed to talk to other girls with ALD who were my age, but I didn't know any. The youngest carrier I knew was my half-sister, who was ten years older than me. While I knew that for the most part she would understand my worries, what I really craved was to meet other teenage carriers like me.

I decided to make a concentrated effort to locate other young ALD carriers. Since ALD is such a rare disease, this wasn't exactly an easy feat. In addition, it seemed that most carriers only learned of their carrier status only after they had a son who got sick and was ultimately diagnosed with ALD. It was exceedingly difficult to find younger females who knew they were carriers. So, I did what most other teenage girls in my situation would do and turned to social media.

I scoured Facebook, and although I found several ALD groups, and even a few groups that were limited to female carriers of ALD, I didn't find any teenage carriers to talk to. I confessed my disappointment to my mom.

"There have to be some other carriers your age out there," she said. "You just have to keep looking. They're probably looking for you too."

I thought a lot about what my mom said. *She's right, maybe there are teenage carriers out there looking for other carriers to talk to.* This prospect prompted me to create my own Facebook group specifically for ALD carriers under age twenty-five. I called the group "Young ALD Carriers," or YAC for short. I posted about YAC on the other carrier Facebook groups I belonged to and encouraged young carriers to join. It wasn't long before requests to join the group rolled in. I created the group's first post:

My name is Taylor Kane. I am a sixteen-year-old ALD carrier. My father died from ALD when I was five, and I've known that I am a carrier since I was very young. I started this group because I feel that young ALD carriers (YACs), as a group, are often overlooked and have very little peer or other support. They are basically ignored by the medical community, do not have access to the latest research on ALD carriers (what little research there is), do not fully understand their reproductive options, and have no one their own age to talk to about emotional ALD carrier-related issues. My goal is to provide a forum for YACs to share their experiences, ask questions, provide emotional support, and make other YAC friends. I will attempt to provide information and/or links to up-to-date information that may be of interest to YACs, and start discussions which will hopefully provide insight into how YACs can be best supported—for example, when and how should girls be informed of their carrier status? Young ALD carriers need to band together so our voices will be heard.

I quickly noticed excitement about YAC growing among the new group members. Young women posted on the group page, introducing themselves and expressing their own concerns about being a carrier. As time went on, more and more young ALD carriers joined the group and began participating. I was not alone!

Not very long after the creation of YAC, I was invited to speak about the issues facing young ALD carriers like myself at several ALD conferences before audiences consisting of both doctors and patients. Grateful for the opportunity to do so, I crafted a PowerPoint presentation focusing on our unique concerns: our worries about developing physical symptoms, our difficulties finding reliable medical information and doctors familiar with ALD, our unanswered questions about their reproductive options, as well as our mental health concerns. Although I was by far the youngest speaker in the room at these conferences, the audiences listened with interest and appreciation. After I spoke, other female carriers invariably approached me—some struggling to walk, a few in wheelchairs—expressing their gratitude that their long-standing concerns were finally being articulated. We were all in agreement that it was time for our voices to be heard.

Currently, nearly five years later, YAC continues to flourish, with more than 120 members from countries all over the world. New members continue to join the group, and the conversations are as engaging as ever. I'd like to think that YAC provides an important service to young women who carry ALD by furnishing them with reliable and up-to-date information about medical advances, reproductive options, and genetic testing, as well as compassion, guidance, support, and hope for the future. Having had the opportunity to talk with many of these young women online and even meet with some of them personally certainly helped allay my anxiety about being a carrier of this horrific disease.

CHAPTER TWENTY-SIX

Staking Out My Future

I could hardly sleep the night before SAT scores were scheduled to be released. Since I knew many colleges placed a great deal of emphasis on these scores, I had worked extremely hard—watching endless videos on test-taking techniques and taking practice test after practice test after practice test. I set my alarm for 4:55 a.m., five minutes before the results were to be posted online. I woke my mom up too, and together we silently walked downstairs to her office.

I pulled up a chair, and we both sat in front of her computer monitor and logged into the website where my scores were to be posted. The next few minutes felt like hours. When the clock hit 5:00 a.m., I quickly refreshed the page. Seconds later my score popped up on the screen.

"Oh my God, I can't believe this," I cried. My mom looked confused. "I worked so hard," I continued, "and it was all for nothing." I hadn't achieved the score I had hoped for, and I felt like my world was crashing down around me. I knew I was being dramatic, but I didn't care. I sobbed louder.

"Taylor, come on, don't cry. Your score is fine. It should be high enough to get into most of the colleges you're looking at . . . Come on, it's not that bad. You can always take the test again. Most people do take it more than once, you know," my mom said, trying to comfort me.

Still, I was disappointed in myself. I knew that my score was technically "above average," but I felt as if I failed since I didn't reach the score I had set as my goal. I understood that the SATs were not a great measure of intelligence for many reasons, but I had always considered myself to be a good test taker, especially due to my strong work ethic and diligent study skills.

I continued crying for the next two hours until I had to start getting ready for school. I knew I would have to take the test again if I wanted to be sure I would get accepted to my top-choice college at the time, The George Washington University. I'd just have to study harder.

And I did. Every night before I went to sleep I spent at least forty-five minutes reviewing vocabulary flash cards, making certain I knew the meaning of words like *archetypal* and *circumlocution*. Words that I would probably never remember, much less use, after the test was over.

Two months later I took the SATs again, and this time was overjoyed to learn that I had achieved my goal, scoring more than one hundred points higher than I had on my initial attempt. My hard work had paid off. For the first time in a while, I felt hopeful for my future.

That year I also became involved in a local organization that was bringing a lot of positivity into my life: the Alice Paul Institute. Alice Paul, who is not as well-known by the general public as she should be, was a leading suffragist in the first-wave feminism movement. She was at the forefront of helping women gain the right to vote in 1920, and drafted the Equal Rights Amendment to ensure equality for women in America (which, sadly, has still not been ratified by Congress). And the coolest part: She grew up in my hometown! In fact, her house, known as Paulsdale, has been preserved as a National Historic Landmark and is used to host leadership development programs for girls and women.

When I learned that there was a program at Paulsdale called the Girls Advisory Council—which met once every month to discuss issues affecting women and girls both in the United States and around the world, to teach leadership, networking, and public-speaking skills, and to advocate for the passage of the Equal Rights Amendment—I quickly signed up. I wanted to meet other girls who believed the same thing I did: that despite what many people think, women and men are still not treated equally, and that gender bias continues to affect women in many facets of their lives—from the economic disadvantages they experience at work to educational inequality to gender-based violence and so on.

It was not extremely popular to be considered a teenage feminist (many of my female peers would go to great lengths to hide their intelligence from boys), and I only had a handful of friends who considered themselves to be such. It concerned me that we did not learn about the history of the women's rights movements in school. In fact, the only woman I remember learning about in history class was Eleanor Roosevelt.

Social media was the vehicle that helped me discover my feminist identity. I increasingly saw posts from political figures, celebrities, and other influencers who brought various women's rights issues to the surface. I realized that I wasn't strange or wrong for feeling angry when men I didn't know made unsolicited remarks about my looks or shouted inappropriate comments at me out of their car windows, or for wanting to be called a leader rather than bossy and opinionated. For as long as I could remember, society had taught me that these were just things that happen to girls, and that I had better get used to them. I never understood why so many of my female friends and acquaintances unquestioningly accepted this state of affairs.

Social media also taught me about the far greater discriminatory and unequal treatment women in developing countries continue to experience. In light of this information, I felt that I could not remain silent. I had to speak out: Gender does not make a person "less than."

And I did speak out. The Girls Advisory Council gave me the perfect platform to do so. Along with other girls from many different high schools, I met with federal and state lawmakers to discuss legislation affecting women, spoke in support of the Equal Rights Amendment at the National Foundation for Women Legislators' Conference, and attended the Day of the Girl Summit at the United Nations. These experiences gave me confidence and showed me that I could actually be part of the change.

One of the women's issues that interested me the most was bias against females in health care. I read about how women had been excluded from clinical trials for decades. Since it had long been assumed that males' and females' bodies were biologically identical and that diseases presented the same way in both sexes, scientists had believed that there was no need to study women separately. Even trials with mice typically utilized male mice only. It was only relatively recently that scientists began to appreciate the fact that males and females' bodies are different and that findings that apply to males do not necessarily apply to females. Indeed, when some clinical trials began to include women, researchers found that the same disease could present very different symptoms in men and women (think heart attacks), and that medications that were effective for men were not always effective—and were sometimes even dangerous—for women.

I also learned that as a result of the lack of clinical data pertaining to females as well as socially ingrained gender biases, women's complaints of pain were frequently ignored or taken less seriously than men's, and often erroneously deemed to be psychosomatic. This not only infuriated me, but it explained why females with ALD were long deemed to be unaffected carriers who simply passed the disease on to their sons. It made me wonder how many women with ALD had been suffering in silence—how many had been told their physical symptoms were all in their minds?

I knew things needed to change, and I had an urge to do something. I just wasn't sure what. I had so much going on in my life at the moment: visiting colleges and serving as president of Hero Club (and several other school clubs as well), as well as interning and volunteering. And of course there was YAC. I promised myself that one day soon I would return to this important issue and educate myself further to see if there was some way I could help make a difference.

I spent my last summer of high school touring different colleges and working on my applications. I also had another important item on my to-do list: helping my mom prepare for her upcoming wedding to my soon-to-be stepdad, Keith. My mom and Keith had started dating during my freshman year in high school. At first, Keith and I didn't exactly have the best relationship, and I was resistant to having him join our family. While I knew he wasn't trying to replace my dad, he quickly imposed new rules that I wasn't used to and often disapproved of my outfits for parties and concerts. (Okay, my outfits might have been a little short or tight, but one thing that my mom had never had an issue with was my clothes.) Over time, though, Keith's sincere concern for my and Matthew's well-being, his kind heart, and his quirky sense of humor eventually won me over. I also realized that despite his somewhat strict standards, he always had my best interests at heart and would do anything for me. In fact, many times he cheerfully agreed to drive me to a friend's house or take me shopping after my mom had refused, claiming that she was too busy. Well, maybe she was, but Keith always had time for me, and by my senior year of high school, I was glad they were getting married.

After visiting The George Washington University (GW for short) in Washington, D.C. for the second time, this time with my mom, Matthew, and Keith, I was absolutely certain it was where I needed to be. After all, my increased interest in women's rights issues had inspired me to become much more politically involved, and GW was in the heart of the action, just a few blocks from the White House. It was widely considered the most politically active college in the nation, and I craved to be surrounded by people who were as passionate as I was about making a difference in the world. It was also very expensive, and I knew for this reason it would be a hard sell when it came to my mom.

On the drive home, I attempted to convince my mom to let me apply. "Mom," I started. "I love GW. I really can't imagine myself going to school anywhere else. I want to apply Early Decision."

"I really liked it too," my mom said. "It's so expensive, though. We'll have to see if you can qualify for some kind of financial aid."

"Okay," I said sullenly.

"I'm sure we can find a way. But you have to apply to other colleges in case you don't get in or we can't afford it."

I promised my mom that I would.

The next few months went by in a blur. Getting accepted to GW was constantly on my mind. It became harder and harder for me to concentrate on anything else. The fact that I had been accepted to several of my back-up schools didn't make me feel any better. I wanted to start a new chapter of my life in Washington, D.C.

On the day GW's acceptance decisions were set to come out, I could hardly sit still. I tried my best to focus during my classes, but it wasn't easy. After school was over, Keith took me to my favorite stationery store to help me pass the time, as I had to wait until 5:00 p.m. for decisions to be posted online. I aimlessly wandered around the store for a while, eventually landing on a notebook I knew I had to buy. On the cover were the words "DREAM BIG" in large gold letters. I was dreaming big alright.

Finally, the moment of truth arrived. Surrounded by my mom, Keith, and Matthew, at five o'clock on the dot, I logged into my GW portal to check the status of my application. With my heart in my throat, I read the word that I had long hoped to see: ACCEPTED.

CHAPTER TWENTY-SEVEN

Remember the Girls

In the fall of 2016, I moved to Washington, D.C. for my freshman year of college, accompanied by several suitcases full of clothes, toiletries, school supplies, and inordinately high expectations. I felt a newfound sense of freedom in the big city and was thrilled that I would be able to make more choices on my own. After all, I was an adult now. I knew that the next four years of my life would be exceedingly important and play a significant role in determining my future. Even though this thought was a bit nerve-racking, I couldn't wait to get started.

My living quarters consisted of an old, relatively small dorm room that teemed with an indeterminant black soot that never went away no matter how many times it was vacuumed or scrubbed. I lived with three roommates, each of whom I had met online through the GW Class of 2020 Facebook page. Our room had a private bathroom, which was a plus, but we couldn't open our closet doors all the way because the room was so crammed with furniture. Still, I paid little attention to my less-than-ideal living situation; I was too busy exploring D.C. with my roommates, attending class lectures, and getting involved in student organizations on campus.

One of my favorite courses was an introductory women's studies course, where I was surrounded by other students who were as passionate about feminism and equal rights as I was. A few weeks into the semester, I couldn't have been more excited to learn that the topic of the day was bias against women in the health care system—the very subject I had promised to come back to as soon as my life had settled down.

We discussed many of the issues I had read about before: the historical omission of females from clinical trials; the long-standing presumption that females were biologically indistinguishable from males when it came to matters of health and disease; the way medical professionals much more often attributed women's complaints of pain or discomfort to hypochondria, hysteria, or some other psychological malady, as compared to men's; and how study after study was revealing that women—still—were being subjected to substandard medical care, being under- or misdiagnosed, made to wait longer for emergency room treatment, prescribed either the wrong medication or the wrong dosage, all because of their gender.

I found the subject matter both captivating and maddening, and for the next few days I couldn't get it out of my head. It was clearer than ever to me that gender bias was the reason, or at least part of the reason, that so many female ALD carriers I had spoken to at conferences and online had resignedly—sometimes angrily—confided that their doctors had informed them that their difficulty balancing, or the tingling in their lower extremities, or their loss of bladder or bowel control, was all in their minds. Certainly not a manifestation of ALD. "Female carriers do not get physical symptoms," these women were told time and time again.

I understood that the doctors and scientists who were researching ALD and trying to find cures had to focus on males with the disease—admittedly, their symptoms were typically more severe than females' symptoms, and often life-threatening. But that didn't mean that women's symptoms should be downplayed or dismissed as though they were nothing. My frustration began to build.

Living in Washington, D.C., gave me easy access to an extensive array of resources, nonprofit organizations, and a community of individuals I had never realized existed, all devoted to treating and curing rare diseases like ALD. Patients, caregivers, and advocates for a multitude of rare diseases came together in an attempt to ignite change and to collectively advocate for laws and regulations benefiting the entire rare disease community. During my sophomore year, I took on a public policy internship at the National Organization for Rare Disorders, a short Uber ride away from my dorm. I also began to attend rare disease summits and conferences and briefings, searching for others who had the same concerns as I did about the inequities in health care when it came to females with rare diseases.

It didn't take long. I quickly met other women, many of whom were carriers of X-linked diseases other than ALD—diseases like hemophilia, Duchenne muscular dystrophy, chronic granulomatous disease, FG syndrome, and Kennedy's disease, which, like ALD, were commonly thought of as "male diseases." These women frequently told me that they too were having difficulty getting doctors to believe that their physical symptoms were real.

During one conference, for example, I was approached by a woman named Brenda who told me that she had both a son and a daughter with hemophilia. She recounted that getting her son diagnosed and placed on a treatment regimen was relatively simple, but that it was far more challenging to arrange care for her carrier daughter.

"Female carriers of hemophilia," Brenda explained, "can have such a low clotting factor that, if they were males, they would be diagnosed with moderate hemophilia and treated accordingly. But since females are still considered by most doctors to be 'simply carriers,' their complaints are often dismissed, and they are refused suitable treatment. Since my daughter is so young, it was extremely difficult for us to find a specialist who took her symptoms seriously. Most doctors won't even see a girl with hemophilia until she begins to menstruate due to the long-held belief that the only indicator of the disease carriers may experience is a heavier-than-normal menstrual cycle. This is just flat out untrue."

Another woman who was herself a manifesting carrier of Duchenne muscular dystrophy contacted me by email after hearing me speak about my YAC group at a conference. She reported that like ALD carriers, carriers of Duchenne were commonly regarded as "just carriers" despite the fact that many of them also developed weakness in their arms and legs and a form of heart disease known as cardiomyopathy. "I just can't stand the fact that female carriers are treated as if they don't exist," she wrote.

I heard similar stories from carriers of a number of other X-linked recessive disorders. While the physical symptoms caused by all of these diseases were different, the women's feelings of frustration and isolation were similar. I realized that as difficult as it was for male rare disease patients to navigate the health care system and find knowledgeable doctors or effective treatments, being a woman with a rare disease was a double whammy.

There really needs to be some type of group or organization that connects women who carry X-linked diseases so that they can join forces and advocate for change, I thought. *If we stand together, we would have a better chance of having our voices heard and challenging the status quo.* After searching for such an organization but finding none, there was only one option: creating my own.

After several months of planning, researching, speaking with other advocates and specialists, and completing complicated business and tax forms, I borrowed several hundred dollars from my mom and founded my own 501(c)(3) nonprofit organization, which I called "Remember the Girls." Its mission: to unite and support women and girls with X-linked recessive disorders through education, support, and advocacy.

While it took a little longer than I would have liked for me to get it up and running (on top of studying, I often work late nights bartending to pay my bills), I am extremely proud of the fact that over the last year, Remember the Girls has grown exponentially. We currently have a twelve-person board of directors consisting of women representing various X-linked disorders, a medical advisory board with several well-qualified doctors and geneticists, and an online support group that serves hundreds of carriers worldwide. Remember the Girls raises awareness about the physical and emotional issues faced by female carriers, provides information about genetic testing and alternative reproduction, advocates for increased attention from the medical community about the physical symptoms carriers may experience, and fights to eliminate the gender inequities in the health care system. We are currently in the process of creating a registry of female carriers to promote and support carrier-focused research, and have several exciting projects in the works to better support our community of women and ensure that future generations of carriers are not overlooked.

Best of all, people are already beginning to listen! Over the last year, I have been invited to speak on behalf of Remember the Girls at a wide variety of medical, scientific and patient advocacy conferences and events across the country and even internationally. I love having the opportunity to educate others about female carriers and the issues that are important to us. While I know we have a long way to go, I can't help feeling extremely optimistic about what we will be able to accomplish. I am looking forward to graduating college next semester and hopefully having more time to devote to not only Remember the Girls, but to the entire rare disease community.

There is no better feeling than discovering your purpose in life. I spent many years searching for my purpose, feeling lost, wondering, *What am I here for?* For a long time after my dad died, I bounced back and forth between serenity and depression, self-assuredness and anxiety, optimism and hopelessness, and faith and fear. This continual tug of war took a huge toll on me. The notion that my life lacked a "purpose" was constantly in the back of my mind. I often felt numb and disconnected from the people I cared about, and wondered if I would ever feel truly happy.

Now, I know I've found my place. Advocating for women and girls with rare diseases has lit a fire inside me. I wake up every day excited to do more.

The people I've met on this journey—children and young adults who have rare disorders or who advocate on behalf of their parents or siblings with rare disorders; parents and grandparents with rare children or grandchildren; strong and unstoppable men and women who tirelessly fight for laws that benefit the rare disease community; doctors and scientists who devote their lives to searching for cures; and of course, my fellow X-linked carriers—are my personal heroes, my inspiration, my extended family.

When you have a rare disease, one that is referred to by a three-letter acronym because it's so difficult to pronounce and so rare that even your doctors have never heard of it, it's easy to feel isolated. Like you are standing alone in a desperate battle against your genes. For a long time I felt as though my dad and I were zebras in a field brimming with horses. But now that I'm surrounded by so many incredible people who are rare like us, I realize that while our stripes may set us apart, they also strengthen us.

EPILOGUE

It's Sunday, June 16, 2019—Father's Day. As is usual on Father's Day, my mom, Matthew, and I (and now Keith too) make the forty-minute trek from our house to the cemetery where my dad is buried. Aside from holiday celebrations, we don't have many real family traditions, but visiting my dad's gravesite on Father's Day, on September 12 (his birthday), and on Christmas Eve, is one tradition to which we've faithfully adhered for the last fifteen years. It's also one I have come to cherish.

After we enter the rustic gate leading to the densely populated cemetery, Keith pulls the car around the bend and parks on the side of the narrow, unpaved road. We step outside, and the warm, bright sun casts a luminous glow on the hundreds of headstones before us, all situated in neat rows on a carpet of newly cut green grass. It feels almost surreal to be surrounded by the stark permanence of death on such a beautiful spring day—a cemetery, I muse, is supposed to feel eerie and cold, like it does when we visit on Christmas Eve and the ground is frozen and the bone-chilling wind prevents us from lingering too long.

My brother and I begin scanning our surroundings for my dad's gravestone. For the first few years after he died, it was easy to find—he was near the end of a row with a wide open field to his left. Now, though, there is no more barren field. His is one in an ever-increasing multitude of headstones, many strewn with flowers—some shaped to form the word "Dad"—and other statuesque trinkets symbolizing this second Sunday in June.

Today we were in a hurry, however, and arrive empty-handed. It feels strange, and somehow sacrilegious, to visit my dad without bringing flowers or some sort of remembrance to leave behind. Last Christmas Eve, I recall, we decorated his grave with a beautiful wreath and a small Christmas tree adorned with gold ornaments and blinking lights. We almost always bring something. Years ago, when Matthew was still a toddler and couldn't fully grasp the fact that our dad was not somehow living under the ground, his little arms would be filled with items he had gathered from our house—cookies, Tastykakes, and even his prized Game Boy—to leave for our dad "so he wouldn't be hungry or bored." My mom gave up trying to explain that this wasn't necessary and would sneak the items back to the car when Matthew wasn't looking.

When we were a little older, we would write letters to my dad and leave them on his grave, along with various stuffed animals or knick-knacks we thought he would like. Today, though, the busy reality of our lives has caught up with us, and we still have to celebrate this day with my PopPop, and then my mom has to get things ready for Keith's Father's Day dinner back at our house.

"We don't need to bring something every single time. Your father would understand," my mom insists.

"But it will look like no one visited him on Father's Day," I sigh.

"It doesn't matter what other people think," she assures me. "Your being here would be enough for him."

We continue searching for my dad, noticing some of the shiny new head-stones, many of which proudly display pictures of those now gone—often beautiful portraits taken in the prime of their lives, before old age, or sickness, or some other misfortune took its toll.

"Why doesn't Daddy's have a picture?" Matthew asks.

"I don't think they had that option when he died," my mom answers. "At least if they did, I never knew about it. They did ask me if I wanted to pay for an extra-deep plot so when I died I could be buried directly on top of him. We would have had a double headstone, which would have been engraved with my name and the year I was born, 1964. I couldn't do it. I was only in my thirties then—I felt like I was too young to have to see my name on a headstone. And I knew the thought would make you guys too upset."

I finally locate my dad's gravestone, in between Mrs. McGuire and Mrs. Kelly, both of whom had passed away in their sixties. My mom always jokes that my dad, who himself was almost 100 percent Irish, is probably having a blast with these two older ladies, whose husbands it seems are still living—both in their nineties.

JOHN J

KANE

SEPT. 12, 1952

DEC. 20, 2003

FOREVER IN OUR HEARTS

We tentatively kneel down on the grass and prepare for another family ritual we have performed for as long as I can remember: taking turns filling our dad in on what we've done and accomplished since the last time we visited—in other words, what he has missed. Although in a way I find this unnecessary since I always feel my dad's presence around me and firmly believe he already knows what is going on in my life and helps guide me through it, it's a nice family bonding experience and it somehow gives me a feeling of serenity.

I always go first.

"Hi, Daddy," I say aloud. "Well, I just finished my junior year at GW. I did really well and I'm actually going to be graduating a semester early. I've been working a lot since school ended, trying to save money for next semester. I had to reschedule my TMJ surgery, but I'll probably reschedule it for some time over fall break. Umm . . . nothing else major going on right now. Everything's good. I miss you."

I have to admit, I do feel a little silly talking aloud to my dad's headstone at my age, but I don't see my mom allowing us to give up this tradition anytime in the near future. I know my brother feels a bit awkward too as he sheepishly begins speaking.

"Hi, Dad. I finished my freshman year at Rowan University. I'm majoring in computer science, and I'm on track to get my masters in three more years. That's it really."

"Maybe you should tell Daddy about your girlfriend," my mom teases.

Matthew rolls his eyes. "Okay, so I have a girlfriend. I'm pretty sure I told him that last time we were here."

My mom smiles. It's her turn. She usually sums up what my brother and I have said in her own protracted way, then adds some comments designed to make sure we leave on a high note.

"Hi, Jack," she begins. "We're all doing fine. Like she told you, Taylor's doing really well at GW. She made the Dean's List again and she loves living in D.C. She's also still working hard to raise awareness of ALD to honor your memory, and she's been devoting a lot of time to her own nonprofit. I know you'd be so proud of her.

"You'd be proud of Matthew too. I'm sure you wouldn't be surprised to hear that he got a perfect 4.0 this year, although I've never seen him study as hard as he did this last semester. I'm pretty sure he enjoyed living in a dorm, although he usually did manage to make it back home almost every weekend with a huge load of wash for me. And you would absolutely love his girlfriend—they are so cute together!

"I've been good too. We miss you . . . Happy Father's Day, Jack."

Having finished her soliloquy, my mom turns to Keith. "Your turn."

Keith has come to visit my dad's grave with us on Father's Day ever since he and my mom were married. He's always been extremely emotional when we gather around the gravestone, and today is no exception. With tears streaming down his cheeks, he addresses my dad.

"Jack," he begins. "I just want to tell you that you have two really special kids. They are both incredible human beings who I have no doubt will make the world a better place. I'm honored that I've had the opportunity to know them and be involved in their lives. I promise you that I'll always do the best I can to make sure that they're safe and taken care of. . . . Happy Father's Day."

I have to smile at Keith's speech. I know without a doubt that my dad would have loved him.

Having each said our piece, Matthew and I crouch behind my dad's head-stone while my mom shoots a picture of us with her cell phone. This is part of our tradition too. I have so many pictures of us in this very position, year after year, beginning when we were both toddlers. To me, the pictures serve as a physical reminder of how big a role my dad still plays in all of our lives, and the fact that no matter how busy we are, we are always a united family. We stare somberly at my dad's grave for a few moments, then slowly walk back to the car. Even today, I get a twinge of guilt every time we leave. It feels like I'm leaving my dad there all alone. "Bye, Daddy," I whisper softly so no one else can hear.

On the ride home, I think about how much I missed my dad's presence when I was growing up. The fact that he died before I ever really got to know him is devastating to say the least. It is heartbreaking. Untenable. I would have done anything to have had him in my life for a little bit longer. To have had him there at my kindergarten graduation . . . smiling up at me from the audience when I played Annie in my second grade musical . . . comforting me after I caught my eighth grade boyfriend cheating on me with one of my best friends . . . taking pictures of me in my sparkly white gown before senior prom . . . cele-brating my eighteenth birthday . . . walking me down the aisle one day. But for all of the pain and sorrow and regret that came with losing my dad, there was some good too—a silver lining. A gift that I had to unwrap, layer by layer, year after year, until I could understand and appreciate it.

I understand now that losing my dad at such a young age taught me compassion. It required me to become resilient and independent. It made me realize how important it is to reach out to help others, and that doing so is the best antidote for one's own grief or loneliness or despair. It reminded me that life is short and if a problem needs fixing, instead of waiting for someone else to come to the rescue, it is up to me to jump in and try to fix it myself. And most important, it showed me that love lasts forever and that the best way to honor the legacy of those who have gone is to continue to live in a way that would make them proud.

And while the gift my dad left behind made me a better person, I know my journey is only just beginning. There are still more layers to unwrap. More challenges to face. More of me to discover. I also know without a doubt that my dad will be beside me, lifting me up, the entire way.

RESOURCES

If you are interested in learning more about or supporting Remember the Girls, the non-profit organization I founded to unite, educate and support females with X-linked recessive disorders, please visit RememberTheGirls.org or email taylor@RememberTheGirls.org.

There are hundreds of charitable organizations and patient advocacy groups which support individual rare disease communities. Listed below are some excellent umbrella organizations.

Global Genes
Website: https://globalgenes.org

Global Genes is a non-profit advocacy organization whose mission is to eliminate the challenges of rare and genetic diseases. It connects, empowers and inspires the rare disease community by raising awareness, providing public and physician education, building community support and funding research to find treatments and cures.

NORD (National Organization for Rare Disorders)
Website: https://rarediseases.org

NORD is a patient advocacy organization dedicated to individuals with rare diseases and the organizations that serve them. It has more than 280 patient organization members, and is committed to the identification, treatment, and cure of rare disorders through programs of education, advocacy, research, and patient services.

EveryLife Foundation for Rare Diseases

Website: https://everylifefoundation.org

The EveryLife Foundation is dedicated to advancing the development of treatment and diagnostic opportunities for rare disease patients through science-drive public policy. It provides the training, education, resources and opportunities for rare disease patients to make their voices heard.

Genetic Alliance

Website: http://www.geneticalliance.org

Genetic Alliance is an international coalition that aims to transform health in the field of genomics research. It is comprised of more than 600 advocacy, research and healthcare organizations that represent the interests of millions of individuals with genetic conditions.

EURORDIS

Website: https://www.eurordis.org

EURORDIS is a non-governmental patient-driven alliance of patient organizations representing 862 rare disease patient organizations in 70 countries. It is the voice of 30 million people affected by rare diseases throughout Europe.

CORD (Canadian Organization for Rare Disorders)

Website: https://www.raredisorders.ca

CORD provides a strong common voice to advocate for health policy and a healthcare system that works for those with rare disorders. CORD works with governments, researchers, clinicians and industry to promote research, diagnosis, treatment and services for all rare disorders in Canada

ORDI (Organization for Rare Disorders India)

Website: https://ordindia.org/

ORDI (www.ordindia.org) is a national umbrella organization representing the collective voice of all patients with rare diseases in India. Its vision is to make rare diseases as easily diagnosed and treated as common diseases like Diabetes, Hypertension, TB and AIDS

ABOUT THE AUTHOR

Taylor Kane is the founder and president of the non-profit, Remember the Girls, an international support and advocacy organization which unites, educates and empowers female carriers of rare genetic disorders--a group which is underrepresented and often overlooked by the medical profession. Taylor learned that she, herself, was a carrier of the rare genetic disease Adrenoleukodystrophy (ALD) after her father died from the disease when she was five years old and has been a fierce advocate ever since, working to raise awareness of the disease as well as funds for ALD research. In 2013, she successfully lobbied the New Jersey legislature and governor to enact a law requiring the screening of newborns for ALD, as the disease can only be cured if treated before symptoms develop.

Taylor is an accomplished speaker, author, and an award-winning activist. She is currently a senior at The George Washington University in Washington, D.C. where she is pursuing a bachelor's degree in Political Communication with a minor in Women's Studies. Taylor calls Mount Laurel, New Jersey home. In her free time she enjoys reading, watching documentaries, and relaxing with her dog, Jynx.

thetaylorkane.com

facebook: @taylorckane